# San Juan River

## A Fly-Angler's Journal

**Richard R. Twarog**

©2006 by Richard R. Twarog

All rights reserved. No part of this book may be reproduced without the
written consent of the publisher, except in the case of brief excerpts in critical reviews and articles.

All inquiries should be addressed to:
Frank Amato Publications, Inc.
P.O. Box 82112 • Portland, Oregon 97282 • 503-653-8108
www.amatobooks.com

Book Design: A.D. Huntsinger
Art Direction and Photography by Richard R. Twarog.

Printed in Singapore
1 3 5 7 9 10 8 6 4 2

Softbound ISBN: 1-57188-373-8
Hardbound ISBN: 1-57188-374-6
Limited Edition Hardbound ISBN: 1-57188-379-7

# Table of Contents

Acknowledgements
4

Dedication
5

Early People in the Americas
7

Early Man in the Southwest
9

Early Man on the San Juan
9

Pueblitos and Navajo Country
10

Spanish, Mexican and Anglo Presence
13

Damming the San Juan River
13

Navajo Dam Gets a Gift
14

You Haven't been to the San Juan if
You Haven't Been to "Abe's"
15

The River
18

Stocking the San Juan
31

The San Juan Worm
35

Midges
38

The Pike of Navajo Lake
42

San Juan River Map
44-45

The Bass of Navajo Lake
48

The Carp of Navajo Lake
52

Fishing for Carp with Chris
55

Meeting Larry—Again
59

A Conversation with Marc Wethington
64

An Interview with
(My Friend) "Bear" Goode
73

A Day with Tom Knopick
77

Fly Recipes
83

## Acknowledgements

This book is not only based on my fishing the San Juan River for years, but also many, many hours of interviews with guides, biologists, scientists, fellow fly-fishers and of course reading volumes of scholarly publications. There is no doubt that without the generosity of my friend Larry Johnson and the following wonderful people I would not even attempt this book.

*Thank you all:*
Keith Burkhart, Tim and Abe Chavez, Professor Bob DuBey, Bill Eaves,
Bear Goode, Harry Gross, Chris and Karin Guikema, Ray Johnston,
Tom Kopnick, Manuel Monasterio, Bob Peltz, Ben Peters, Tracy Peterson,
Marc Wethington, and Richard Youngers.

The beautiful "Richard's In-Country" was tied by Richard Youngers.

The original "San Juan Worm" was tied by its creator, Bob Pelzl.

The "Richard's San Juan Worm" and the "Richard's Midge Emerger" were tied by the author along with the "Clouser Fly."

All of the other beautiful flies were tied by my friend and master tier—Tracy Peterson.

All photographs by the author.

This book is dedicated to my fellow Vietnam Veterans.

*Richard's In-Country*

I designed the body of the fly to replicate the Vietnam Service Medal
with the black and white of the wing, hackle and tail
representing the MIA flag.

# The First People in the Americas

The San Juan River in New Mexico is one of the ten *great* rivers in North America. When you visit, and become a guest of this river, and behave as a guest, the San Juan becomes a fabulous host—graciously welcoming you.

This book is about fly-fishing the San Juan River and its impoundment. Being that the San Juan drainage is loaded with prehistory and history of early Americans, I am including a tiny bit of anthropological information for those readers interested in the area they fish in.

When the last ice age was at its peak, and the glaciers were completely formed 14,000 to 20,000 years ago, much of the earth's water was locked up in mile-high ice sheets in the Northern Hemisphere; worldwide, sea levels were 300 feet lower than today, exposing the massive, unglaciated, so-called land bridge between what is now Asia and North America. Lowering the sea level only 100 feet would join the two continents.

As the glaciers melted, the sea rose and flooded the land bridge. From that time on, migration was by some type of floating vessel, or by long walks on top of slabs of floating ice. Today the depth of the Bering Strait ranges between 98 to 164 feet—so shallow that it often freezes solid in the winter. Indeed, the Inuit people travel over the frozen ice between Siberia and Alaska to visit relatives. The Bering Strait theory proposes adventurous (very macho male) Asian hunters followed their meals-on-the-hoof, herds of bison, mammoths and mastodons as they grazed. This assumes, of course, that the "land bridge" was covered with mega flora—enough grasses to attract these grazing mega fauna. Remember, the bison (eight feet at the shoulder) and mammoths were huge; they needed a lot of food. I must say, the spectacle of short men (not quite 5 feet tall) armed with short-spears chasing down a bunch of elephants ( today's Asian elephants can bounce along at about 16 mph) is quite interesting. Personally, I would have run after wild turkeys. They migrated at the same time. And they don't fight back as hard.

Anthropologists and archeologists have been telling us this is what happened at least 11,500 years ago. And, they have fossils with spear points still imbedded in the bones, or next to them, of these giant pre-historic elephants (mammoths and mastodons) and bison, to prove it in archaeological sites in Wyoming, Colorado, Arizona and New Mexico. The hunters are called the Clovis People. The culture (the people) and the points are named after Clovis, New Mexico, the town near the first archeological finding. The Clovis hunters invented the Clovis point, where form met function: these hunters crafted astonishingly beautiful double-fluted, lethally sharp, projectile points.

And they also invented the first weapons system—the *atlatl* and the dart—essentially a short-spear and its launcher thrower. A kind of whip-lash force is added when the spear or dart is put on top of a grooved board. The board (the *atlatl*) is held in one hand with the six-foot dart on top. The hunter would then "throw" the dart with a kind of tennis racket serve, sending the dart at least 120 yards. With practice came accuracy. The combination of the *atlatl* and the double-fluted projectile point were the epitome of high-tech weaponry. The bow and arrow replaced the *atlatl* about A.D. 600.

Another method of hunting the Clovis People used was very deadly, too deadly, and not very sporting—they stampeded bison and mastodon over cliffs, young and old alike, entire matriarchal herds were slaughtered and then butchered on the spot. These bison were at least a third larger than present-day bison. How much meat can short men carry? How much was just plain wasted, just left behind to rot in the hot Southwest sun? Some experts think that drought plus the Clovis People's weapons system plus their propensity to overkill, precipitated the extinction of the mega fauna.

The traditional Bering Strait hypothesis continues: the first immigrants (Paleo-Indians) to what is now the Americas were from Mongoloid stock. Groups of perhaps 10 to 50 people migrated in waves for a few hundred years over the exposed 55 miles of land (Beringia) of the Bering Strait between what is now Siberia and Alaska during the last ice age (the Pleistocene). This exposed land bridge was no Verrazano, George Washington or Golden Gate, as long as they are they cannot compare in size. The "bridge" was over one thousand miles wide. Really, it wasn't a bridge at all: it was an isthmus joining two continents.

Our "bridge" didn't have a toll collector, so travel flowed freely in both directions. Many species from Asia walked over—bison, turkeys, dogs, caribou, deer, elk, moose and elephants came to this continent; camels and horses passed them on their way to Asia. This was not a Noah's Ark deal. They didn't all travel at the same time to the same place. Some today, and some a few months later, and so on, for many hundreds of years.

Textbooks say Asians of Mongoloid stock started crossing the Bering Strait into North America 11,500 years ago qualifying them as the first Stone Age Americans. Guess what? The Stone Age South and North Americas were not devoid of humans 11,500 years ago. There were already people here to greet those who came by the Bering Strait land bridge. There is an archeological site in South America that dates back 12,500 years ago; one in Pennsylvania back 12,000 years ago at minimum, maybe even back 17,000 years ago; and there's a site in Virginia that dates back 14,000 years ago. People came from South Asia, East Asia and even—gasp—Europe. (Probably from the Iberian Peninsula.) They were here long before Leif Ericson made his trip. So, obviously, as Dennis Stanford of the Smithsonian Institution said "…we are looking at multiple migrations through a very long time period—migrations of many different peoples of many different ethnic origins." According to the National Geographic Society, he and others believe it's important to explore the hypothesis that Europeans participated in the first settling of the Americas.

Distinctive adaptive systems to a specific environment such as language, burial customs, food acquisition, social organizations, tools (like the Clovis point), and dwellings, to name just a few, distinguish—and separate—one group

*Petroglyphs can be looked at as representational: art not as a specific word or part of any particular language, but rather, conveying a meaning of an episode that occurred during the artist's experience or through oral legend. Or, they can simply be trail markers—a kind of street sign or landmark. I would never have found the hundreds of petroglyphs in the canyons of Gobernador if I weren't guided by my friend Ray Johnston—a lifelong resident.*

of the same race from another. Anthropologists call these differences "cultures." There were many different isolated groups and cultures throughout the Americas. Though the Clovis people were not the first immigrants to the Americas they are among the earliest people we have record of in the Southwest. Let's stay with early man in the Southwest.

## Early Man in the Southwest

Where Arizona, Colorado, New Mexico, and Utah meet, is called the Four Corners; between about A.D. 700 and A.D. 1400 it was the most cosmopolitan and densely developed area in North America. However, it was hardly a melting pot: the different groups fought with each other, taking slaves, mostly children and women, and anything of value. And they continued to fight with each other up to and after their contact with Europeans.

The Anasazi were a nomadic people living in natural caves or quickly-made, very simple shelters. Between A.D. 500 to A.D. 700 they started making stone-lined pits in the floors of caves and stored their newly acquired maize in them. About the same time they started building larger storage pits, adding walls of stone and poles with a roof of brush. Sometimes they used mud as a sort of plaster.

Then, between A.D. 700 to about A.D. 1,000 the Anasazi built one-story houses above ground with connecting rooms. Somewhere around A.D. 1,000, they built multi-story dwellings with contiguous rooms, many set high in canyon walls, such as Mesa Verde. The architecture wasn't especially sophisticated or innovative. The small rooms were built with rocks and baked mud, using a roof of logs resting on horizontal timbers. By the end of the 13th century these cliff dwellings were deserted. As were other buildings in an area spanning from Flagstaff, Arizona to Pagosa Springs, Colorado. The Anasazi were the precursors to the current Pueblo Indians. (Currently there are about 50,000 Pueblo Indians living in Arizona and New Mexico speaking at least eight different languages.)

*Possible birthing scene.*

As I said, since this is a book about fly-fishing the San Juan River in New Mexico, not anthropology, I'm skipping a few traditions and cultures to focus on the Navajo Dam area where the famous San Juan River fishery is. So let's move on and talk a little about the history of the inhabitants along this section of the San Juan River in New Mexico.

## Early Man on the San Juan

The sandstone and shale rock formations surrounding Navajo Lake were deposited 50 million years ago. Federally mandated site excavations before construction of Navajo Dam began in 1958 revealed some evidence of humans (Clovis hunter-gatherers) from 6,000 B.C. to A.D. 1.

However, the majority of the sites encompassed pre-Pueblo and Pueblo periods (A.D. 200 to as late as, optimistically, A.D. 1300). The early Pueblo Indians were replaced in roughly 100 years by the ancestors of the modern Navajo and the Apache and Ute. These Athabascan-speaking peoples—the future Navajo and Apaches—showed up near the present site of Navajo Lake sometime in the 1400's. They split into many different groups. The Shoshonean-speaking ancestors of the Utes appeared nearby at what would become the north end of Navajo Lake, the southwest corner of Colorado.

*This is a figure of Monster Slayer resplendent with tools of his trade to the left (his right). Monster Slayer is one of numerous Navajo deities.*

*This Ye'i represents the deity of harvest and the deity of plenty and the deity of mist. It holds a digging stick for planting seed. It also wears a set of mountain sheep horns and a feathered hump (probably eagle) that contains seeds and moisture for planting. This petroglyph was carved in the wall of Crow Canyon, near the San Juan River.*

(Meanwhile, elsewhere in the world, in 1543 in Crakow, Poland, Nicholas Copernicus, was advancing the heliocentric theory that the sun was the center of the universe and the earth revolved around it. Leonardo da Vinci finished his brilliant creation, the Portrait of Mona Lisa in 1504. And Michelangelo's 14' 3" colossal sculpture of David chiseled from gorgeous white marble. And, of course, Michelangelo's uniquely grand Sistine Chapel ceiling. Around 1696, in Europe, Sir Isaac Newton had already invented integral calculus and defined the laws of motion and universal gravitation which were able to be printed thanks to Johannes Gutenberg and his moveable-type press completed around 1440.)

## Pueblitos and Navajo Country

Of the ancestral groups, the nascent Navajos left the most information about themselves close to the dam site. Sometime between 1500 and 1700 the Navajo moved into the canyons of the Gobernador region just a few miles from the present-day Navajo Dam. There they built "pueblitos": modest, simple, stone fortresses hidden high among the cliffs and boulders. Blending into their landscape without effort. These were brutal, turbulent times: some pueblitos were fortresses built to shelter families, the elderly, and spiritual leaders from raids by the Navajo's many enemies; and some served as lookouts and signaling sites, ostensibly to warn other pueblitos of marauding tribes or Spaniards trying to capture their livestock and slaves.

There are many ruins of abandoned pueblitos in the area. One is near Simon Canyon overlooking the San Juan River. I've seen one on a cliff face of the Los Pinos arm of Navajo Lake. Another close one is in Frances Canyon near the Navajo Dam. That one's first rooms were built around 1710. We know from dendrochronolgy that construction continued episodically through the early 1740's. The first-floor trapdoor led to an escape route and there was a tower-lookout with holes that could be used by defenders

*It must have been a successful hunt.*

to fire at approaching enemies. By all outward appearances pueblitos were built to provide a strong defense. Obviously, with good reason, many skeletons have been unearthed without heads or with projectile points embedded in them.

Gobernador Knob is considered to be the "heart" of Navajo country. The Knob is southeast of Navajo Dam. It is the birthplace of the Navajo deity, Changing Woman. According to Navajo mythology, her name comes from the cycle of changes in her age: young in the spring, mature in the late summer, old in winter, and young again the following spring. The Hero Twins, of Navajo mythology, Monster Slayer and Born of Water, are progeny of Changing Women, also called in some myths Mother Earth. The twins made their home at what was the confluence of the Los Pinos and San Juan rivers now under the Navajo Lake.

Interestingly, the Navajo creation myth has the Dineh emerging from the underworld in Island Lake seven miles west of Silverton, Colorado in the La Plata Mountains, the northern boundary of sacred Navajo land.

We know the Navajos camped, farmed and hunted along the San Juan River and by the late 17th century, they had started to acculturate to some of the ways of the Spanish. By the mid-1800's, their semi-nomadic lifestyle had changed into a pastoral one with the acquisition of sheep from the Spanish (through raids) and contact with the Pueblo Indians. In the 19th century, they learned silver work from the Spanish. Reservations for the Utes, the Jicarilla Apaches and the Navajo were established in close proximity to present-day Navajo Lake in the period from 1868 to 1870. All three tribes have water rights to the San Juan River.

*Gobernador Knob is considered to be the "heart" of Navajo country. The Knob is southeast of Navajo Dam and is the birthplace of the Navajo deity, Changing Woman.*

*This Pueblito is in Frances Canyon very near Navajo Lake. Built around 1710, it was intermittently occupied until the early 1740's. It's a large complex with a lookout tower and three floors, each with many small rooms and with a trap door into a cellar. It was a formidable defense against real or imagined enemies.*

## SPANISH, MEXICAN AND ANGLO PRESENCE

Spanish and Mexican traders and explorers entered the area in the 18th century. The Dominguez-Escalante expedition from Santa Fe traveled through the northern end of the present-day Navajo Lake area in 1776 leaving a track that would become part of the Old Spanish Trail used by traders on their way to California.

By the 1870's Anglo and Hispanic prospectors, ranchers and farmers started pouring into northwest New Mexico, an area previously off limits until Indian reservations were carved out with defined boundaries. Spanish settlers made homes in the present-day Navajo Lake area. (The little town of Rosa later gave its life for the Navajo Dam in 1962 as it was inundated and its townspeople relocated.) In the 1880's a railroad line from Durango, Colorado went through the present-day lake area on its way to Chama, New Mexico.

## DAMMING THE SAN JUAN RIVER

Private irrigation canals were the only means of bringing precious water to the arid land. Terrible spring flooding and episodic droughts injected drama into humdrum lives. Not surprisingly, dreams of damming the San Juan River (once known as the "Rio de Nabahoo") got more serious in the late 1890's. Brothers Jay and Guy Turley assiduously surveyed the Navajo Dam/Lake area to be and drew maps to tempt investors to finance a dam, but alas, they were ahead of their time and abandoned hope by 1909. Continuing big floods and the need for a predictable water supply kept the dream viable until its incarnation in Navajo Dam in 1962.

In the meantime, the 1922 Colorado River Compact apportioned the Colorado River between upper and lower Colorado River Basin states. Then in 1948 Arizona, Colorado, New Mexico, Utah and Wyoming (the upper basin states) agreed to an allocation of the Colorado River among themselves and by that act carved out New Mexico's share of the San Juan River—a tributary of the Colorado River. Navajo Dam was on the horizon.

Ah, Western water politics—but that's a story worthy of a novel. What I can say is that it wasn't until 1956 that the planets were aligned, a deal was struck and federal monies were finally appropriated to build a dam to deliver irrigation water to Navajo farmers miles away. Admittedly, there were other reasons for damming the San Juan River, but making 110,000 acres of Navajo land arable, was the deal-maker. Navajo Dam and later Glen Canyon Dam dramatically altered the temperament of the San Juan River and were early showpieces of the Colorado River Storage Project.

Even before Navajo Dam was dedicated in 1962 and water began flowing into Navajo Lake, 4 miles of Colorado state highway and 6.5 miles of the Denver and Rio Grande Western railroad track had to be relocated and 50 families moved before their homes were inundated. Huge quantities of local earth and rock went into a dam as high as a 40-story skyscraper. A hydroelectric power plant would be added at the southern base of the Navajo Dam in the late '80's that, thankfully, didn't alter the tailwater trout fishery.

From 1962 to 1991, the Bureau of Reclamation (the BOR) operated the dam to maximize water storage and minimize flow variation below the dam. Spring flows were reduced, flooding was reduced and flows were supplemented in other seasons. Since then, two native fish, the razorback sucker and the Colorado pikeminnow, have been designated as endangered species. Now the BOR has to factor in habitat development downstream below Farmington, New Mexico for the two natives. Fishing remains wonderful in the river and in the lake, Western water politics notwithstanding.

Since the building of Navajo Dam, the San Juan tailwater runs cold and clear. It is designated "quality fishing water," and has special fishing regulations. It's one of this country's top ten trout rivers. I think it's number one.

## Navajo Dam Gets A Present
*By Molly Twarog*

January 6, 1963, four months after Navajo Dam was dedicated, the citizens of the little town of Aztec, New Mexico broke ground on a shortcut road going west to link them to State Highway 511, the road to Navajo Lake. They pitched in to build what would become State Highway 173 so they wouldn't have to go to Navajo Lake by way of Ignacio, Colorado.

A local county commissioner secured a 200-foot right-of-way for a 20-mile road that would run east of Aztec through semi-arid BLM land, home to cottontails, mule deer and oil and gas wells. This "Navajo Dam Road" was built through public donation of lunches, labor, time, talent, and loan of heavy equipment. The Aztec Jaycees partnered this undertaking with local construction companies, the Rotary Club, the Lions, the VFW, the Chamber of Commerce and on and on.

By the 26th of April, 1963, Aztec's earth movers and shakers were done. Their new road was formally transferred to the State of New Mexico at a ceremony during—what else, in April, in New Mexico—a sandstorm.

Aztec held one more fund-raiser in May—really more a party for themselves from the sound of it. As reported in the *Aztec Independent Review*, "The Dam Follies" showcased all manner of local talent that night—a chorus, skits, fire twirlers, organ music and piano music. The National Municipal League understandably selected Aztec, New Mexico as one of eleven All-American Cities for 1963 in recognition of outstanding boosterism.

Aztec won't forget one person in particular that helped build the road—that's Bonnie Wall, the chairman of the lunch committee. Outside town where lunches were brought to the workers, Bonnie had a rock named for her. Locals know it as "Bonnie's Rock," but don't look for a roadside marker.

## You Haven't Been to the San Juan if you Haven't Been to "Abe's"
*By Molly Twarog*

"When I look at the history of it, I don't even know how they made it—they worked like mules," Tim Chavez says about his parents, Abe and Patsy Chavez. Abe Chavez is one of those "lucky" guys: he was at the right place at the right time, but oh, by the way, he worked hard and long and didn't know he could fail. Abe Chavez and his family businesses—grocery store, motel, gas station, restaurant, boat sales and storage, sporting goods store, fishing guide service—have been at the crossroads of life at Navajo Dam all along.

Abe Chavez can't sit still for long during our conversation in his restaurant one afternoon in October. He's frequently on his feet illustrating one of his stories. His face is animated, he's into it, reliving his deal with his cousin Esther for her fishing pole or fishing the San Juan for suckers and catfish as a boy with his dad. You can easily believe he took a Bantam Weight Golden Gloves title back in 1950, emulating his father, Abie, a professional prizefighter in the Rocky Mountains in the 1920's. With son Tim at his side, Abe revels in talking about his good fortune and the business decisions that panned out so well for him.

We knew the remains of the town of Rosa lay beneath Navajo Lake, but now, ironically, we learn the burial site of Abe's great-grandfather Ulibarri had been at Rosa. In 1958, before river water was impounded, the Bureau of Reclamation moved the graves of Senor Ulibarri and some other Rosa residents to an area behind the landmark white church on the road to Texas Hole. Abe's roots go back to some of the first Hispanic settlers in southern Colorado and northern New Mexico. Ancestors of Abe's were

*Tim and Abe Chavez*

named in old Spanish land grants. In other words, Abe's family was here well before the U.S. gained possession of the New Mexico Territory from Mexico.

Aware that Navajo Dam was about to be built, and fishermen would be drawn to the area, Abe and his wife Patsy moved from Farmington, New Mexico, in 1958, to start their business.

Abe sets the scene. "I borrowed $1,500 from my Aunt Tina. I bought 1 1/2 acres along State Highway 511. I bought a small building for a store for $400 and hauled it from Farmington. Then I bought a trailer house to live in. I was down to $300 and no fishing yet. We didn't even have electricity in the little store, so I bought a couple of Coleman lanterns. I kept one inside and I rigged one outside with a big old stick to get attention at night. I got a refrigerator that was gas. I figured I'd sell cokes and coffee and doughnuts to the dam's construction workers. But when they started building, the cars just zoomed by going to the dam. We were bringing in about $5 and $10 a day. I knew we had to do something to bring them here.

"Guess what! Morrison-Knutson had 700 men working on the dam. So what the company would do was drive into Farmington, bring all the mail out, and distribute it to the guys. That was a headache for Morrison-Knutson, and it cost them money. They knew they had to do that for five years. *They needed a post office up here.* Our little store was about six miles from the dam.

"My dad and the Republican chairman in Farmington went way back. Pretty soon Patsy and I got word that we had won the post office contract. Next day 700 employees up at the Dam were told their mail was here at our little store. That evening people started coming. My wife and I would have coffee for all the workers. So, what happened was, our store became the trading place; that brought us a

*The famous "Abe's," the first business and post office on the San Juan River was established here by Abe Chavez.*

lot of business, you know. That lasted for five years—all those guys were our customers; they were buying gas and snacks from me. After five years they completed the dam—they worked day and night. When they left, I wanted to build a motel."

After the dam was completed in 1962, Abe went on to build a complex of businesses at his present location on State Highway 173, spurred on by increasing numbers of fishermen coming to Navajo Lake and the famous fishery-to-be, the San Juan River tailwater. As savvy a businessman as Abe Chavez is, he couldn't have predicted how good fishing would become. But I get ahead of myself.

Abe counts himself "lucky" his dad taught him the building and plastering trades. (Abe built, plumbed, wired and maintained a succession of motel units, a store and his house over the years.) Lucky? Yeah, that's the "luck" that hard work and having a vision can bring. And while Abe and his wife were running their business and raising a family, Abe was teaching himself more and more about the river.

About the very early days, Abe says, "Game and Fish poisoned the suckers and the squawfish." And casting his vote on today's eco-politics, he added, "We made a big mistake: we let some get away!" Finishing his story, "Then Game and Fish stocked the river with trout while the dam was being built."

Before the quality water became the Quality Water, Abe caught his first four-pound rainbow trout at the spillway. "It looked like a football—that was big news in 1964 or 1965." And, no surprise, Abe can tell you how the Texas Hole got its name. As Abe tells it, Red Means, a salesman for Amarillo Hardware, nailed the future shrine of the San Juan. "He was selling me stuff—salmon eggs, lures and flies and he said to me, 'Abe, you ought to go over to that big hole up there. I call it the Texas Hole because all of the Texans are fishing with garlic cheese!' So, before you knew it, we started calling it the Texas Hole."

When you talk to locals about those days in the '60's on the San Juan, they roll their eyes and ask if you've heard about the San Juan Shuffle or the infamous Rattling Rainbows. Naturally, I go to Abe to find out what the heck they're talking about.

Abe chuckles about the so-called San Juan Shuffle. "We were fishing below the Texas Hole and nothing was hitting. About five cows crossed the river and the fish went crazy. My dad said, 'You don't think them cows had anything to do with it?' I said, 'Nah, how could that have anything to do with it?' But they did. My dad sent me to chase the cows back because he figured out the cows were stirring up the bugs. That was the San Juan Shuffle, little did we know."

As it turned out, the Rattling Rainbows epithet was coined during the time when snails were a terrifically

*Our Lady of Guadalupe Church—a landmark to find the Texas Hole parking lot.*

abundant food source for the fish. Abe's son, Tim, offers, "In 1968 when the first article came out on the river—I think it was in *Outdoor Life*—there was this article called 'Rattlers on the San Juan' that talked about how you can catch these fish and kind of shake them and almost hear the snails." For emphasis Tim holds up his dad's pictures of those fish with huge bellies.

Over the years, the New Mexico Department of Game and Fish biologists invited Abe along when they electro-shocked fish to track changes in the fish population; sometimes he looked along with them at the contents of fish stomachs. With no false modesty Abe says, "I didn't have any degree or nothing, but I got to be pretty good at knowing these fish." Abe became a go-to guy on the river as newspaper and magazine sportswriters frequently turned to him to ask those burning questions—"What're the fish hitting on?" "How's the fishing this year compare to past years?" etc. To this day, the largest-circulation newspaper in New Mexico, the *Albuquerque Journal*, queries "Abe's" for the largest catch of the week.

It's time to pack up the tape recorder and let the restaurant become a restaurant again. About 60 years ago a boy had a dream—to open a little store with fishing supplies like the one his dad and he used to visit in Colorado. Abe and Patsy Chavez turned his dream into a destination roadside business known to tens of thousands of us as just, "Abe's." Some people have all the luck.

## THE RIVER

The San Juan River travels through segments of New Mexico and Utah from its source high in the San Juan Mountains in southwest Colorado, finally joining the Colorado River on its way to Lake Powell. More than likely it got its name from

*Knee-deep snow didn't stop us hiking into the East Fork headwaters of the San Juan to this spot a few miles east of Pagosa Springs, Colorado.*

the Spanish who were in this area around 1765. Don Juan Maria de Rivera gets the credit for naming the San Juan. Commissioned by the head of the Spanish government, in what is now Santa Fe, New Mexico, Rivera went in search of silver and gold and probably slaves.

The San Juan River tailwater is a magnificent fishery; however, it has not always been this way. Before the Navajo Dam was built, this pre-tailwater was a slow-moving, warm and silty river. The only fish you could catch were channel catfish and a few suckers. The dam impounded water from many little tributaries that flow into three main rivers: the Los Pinos, Piedra and San Juan. Creation of a fly-fisherman's paradise was complete three months after the dedication in September, 1962 when 10-inch rainbows were planted for the first time. Now, the temperature of the water flowing from the bottom of the dam is consistently in the low forties and, of course, it's a classic tailwater known worldwide.

Things have changed here since 9/11. Fishing no longer starts at the bottom of the dam. Now it starts from the downstream end of the large island just below the dam. From there, downstream about 100 yards, to the overhead cable that is stretched across the river is the new catch-and-release-only area. The river in this area is wide and slow moving. Here you can find shallow flats, a few small but deep pools and some riffles. This is the coldest water of the river: a very, very cold 40 degrees Fahrenheit.

There's a nice main channel on the northern side that is perfect for black or purple Woolly Buggers and Bunny Leech patterns. There are some really big fish in this area. Wading here, and for that matter, the rest of the river, can be a treacherous. There are some deep drop-offs. And the algae that are so benevolent in giving us lots of bugs is really a mixed blessing. It's slippery. Killer slippery.

*Flashback Pheasant Tail.*

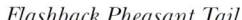

The next downstream area is the Cable Hole. As the name implies, this area starts at the overhead cable and runs downstream about 100 yards. From the cable downstream about 3 1/4 miles special regulations apply: there is a one-fish-over-twenty-inches limit. You must leave the Quality Water and stop fishing if you decide to take that one twenty-incher. (I hope you keep fishing.) There are some riffles beneath the cable. From this pool downstream to the Upper Flats, the water has deep holes and ledges in the sandstone bottom with the main current running near the north bank.

The Upper Flats is a wide section of slow-moving river with a few islands and channels. When the flow is slow, below 600 cfs, it's a great place to wade. The south bank has the slowest water with lots of midges. This is an area with great mayfly habitat.

Just before the river spills into Texas Hole is an area called Kiddie Hole. This is another extremely popular spot. There are dozens of easily seen (with polarized glasses) trout. Besides the number of fish, another attraction to this area is its easy access from the parking lot. There's a path from the eastern (upstream) side of the parking lot that puts you right at the hole. Kiddie Hole has a smooth bottom and is very easy to wade.

Texas Hole—that's where you hit the largest populations on the river. Lots of fish, lots of fishermen. This is the 200 yards of water that many flyfishers come to fish. Or, at least to see before moving on to other parts of the river. This is the deepest and fastest water in the river. Texas Hole begins a bit like a "plunge pool", that is, there are two riffles pouring into the head of the pool forming the main current and a small run coming into it from the north. The head of the pool is about 13 feet deep depending on the flow. Remember this river is very cold and this hole is swift and deep. One false step and …

*Fishing for Colorado River cutthroat on Quartz Creek, one of the feeder streams to the East Fork of the San Juan River in the San Juan River National Forest in Colorado.*

There are large eddies on the north and south sides of Texas Hole. The seams of these eddies are favorites of mine for sliding my midge emerger into the foam. I wait and watch looking for the nose of a sipping trout to come up. Or, you can try a Griffith's Gnat in the seams. You really can't miss the seam and eddy on the south (parking lot side) of the river. Just walk straight to the river on the path from the parking lot. Once there, you'll see riffles on your right, most of that water veers into the main channel and the rest goes straight and creates the eddy. During low flow you can cross the river about 100 yards up from Texas Hole. You may find that it's less crowded on the north side. The head of Texas Hole is also a good area for Brassies, Copper John's and Flashback Pheasant Tails in sizes 22 to 18.

A relatively uncrowded place to fish Texas Hole is right at the put-in. Just follow the dirt road from the parking lot downstream. The put-in is a great place for Woolly Buggers and Bunny Leeches. And people sloshing around don't bother these fish, they'll swim to within a few feet of you. Don't let that fool you, all the trout in the upper river have Ph.D's in homo sapien biology with a minor in the science of tippet extrusion. They can tell a 4X from a 7X from nine yards away, I swear.

The main channel of the Lower Flats continues on the north side of the river. Usually this is fished with a two-fly rig and fished deep. This rather wide, slow, spot has a silty bottom—perfect habitat for midges. Try hoppers here in the summer and early fall.

The Lower Flats leads to Lunker Alley. Now that name conjures up images of big fish just waiting to trounce, devouring anything in their path. My friend, the head guide at Float'N Fish, "Bear" Goode, guided a lucky client into a nice 31 1/2-inch brown trout. Now that's a really nice brown trout! Caught it on a Big Bear Beatis size 20.

*The West Fork of the San Juan River flowing from the San Juan Mountains, north of Pagosa Springs, Colorado.*

*The Upper Flats with the dam on the left.*

*This view is from the north side of the river with the Upper Flats on the bottom left looking downstream towards Baetis Bend on the upper right. Texas Hole begins a bit like a "plunge pool", that is, there are two riffles pouring into the head of the pool forming the main current and a small run coming into it from the north. The head of the pool is about 13 feet deep depending on the flow. With just 200 yards of water, the world-famous Texas Hole has the largest population of trout on the river.*

This hole has two names: Last Chance because it's the last hole before the take-out (which is just to the right of the photograph) and Crusher because there's a very large rock—I stood on it to take this photograph—that can crush a drift boat going too fast during a high runoff. I caught a nice 24-inch rainbow right where the fisherman is standing. By the way, it's also the end of the Quality Water.

*Fall at Cottonwood Campground.*

*Mark Nesbit on the north side at the bottom of Texas Hole getting in a few last casts before the sun sets.*

*This big tough guy was fooled by a tiny size 22 Midge Emerger.*

Again, the main channel continues along the north bank. Lunker Alley is a place for 12-foot leaders and some weight. These are very selective fish: be patient. Try a cone head Woolly Bugger or a Bunny Leech pattern. On either side of the main current there are some nice eddies with accompanying seams.

Moving downstream, there are some absolutely beautiful heavy riffles at Simon Canyon. The water here is a little warmer than upstream and as the water temperature increases in the San Juan, so too, do the numbers of browns. According to Marc Wethington, a marine biologist for the State of New Mexico, the largest caddis hatches happen here in summer and fall. One of the nice things about

*About 8 miles downstream looking towards the village of Las Vegas de San Juan.*

*ET Rock looking upstream. I've seen plenty of beautiful and big rainbows hanging around the quiet waters near the rock just waiting to pounce on the passing food.*

Simon Canyon is you can reach it from the north side. Take your first right after you cross Abe's Bridge, just drive past the Cottonwood Campground and keep going about a mile. You'll find a small parking area and picnic tables right at the canyon.

One way to avoid the crowds is to fish the so-called, "bait water." Fly-fishers make a big mistake by not fishing below the Quality Waters. I caught my biggest rainbow there. Years ago while I was fishing at Crusher Hole, a little downstream from the Quality Water boundary, I saw a little movement in a foam line right at the edge of a seam. Sure enough, trout were feeding on midges that

*AK Callibaetis.*

*Griffith's Gnat.*

were trapped in the foam—the trout were coming out of the water a little, kind of like a whale sounding. And they were also just sipping, taking their time. I drifted my midge emerger into the foam line and BINGO! I landed a nice rainbow. How big? Nose to tail, 25 1/2 inches. Not too shabby. Then I did it again. And again! They weren't all over 20 inches, but they were all over a foot long. Point is, there are fish throughout this river. "Bait water" doesn't preclude fly-fishing.

You can float downstream for another five miles. Private water starts about one mile from Abe's Bridge. There you can float the water, but you can't drop anchor or get out and wade without permission from the landowners. They own the land under the water.

There's just too much water to fish in one day. Take a few days—hire a guide for the first day to introduce you to this beautiful river, find a couple of spots you like, and return and explore. Remember: Twenty-Inch Trout On a Size Twenty Hook.

### STOCKING THE SAN JUAN

The San Juan cannot depend on natural reproduction to replenish its rainbow population. Marc Wethington told me that in October 2001, over 56,000 hybrid trout five to seven inches long were planted in Texas Hole. All these trout were tested for whirling disease 60 days prior to planting. All were disease free.

*Downstream looking towards the town of Blanco with Teetering Rock in the foreground. This is the mesa that is the background of the cover photograph with Ben Peters.*

These are very special trout: a mixture of Eagle Lake, Donaldson trout and steelhead. Eagle Lake trout are a very hearty strain that does very well in the wild even in water that is a little alkaline. Donaldson are trout of enhanced size, strength and rate of growth compared to other rainbows. Sometimes called "super trout" these fish reach sexual maturity in two years instead of the usual four years, and they weigh more and produce more eggs then other rainbows. Of course, we all know the strength and tenacity of steelhead. Can you imagine a better combination?

Brown trout were stocked in the early '60's and continue to be a self-sustaining population. Marc Wethington told me, "The browns came from all over. There is a lot of variation. They're a mishmash of strains." Snake River cutts were also planted about the same time. Since then they also crossbred—you'll probably catch as many cutt-bows as you will rainbows.

In 1998 the New Mexico Game and Fish counted 80,000 fish in the four miles or so of Quality Waters below the Navajo Dam. Imagine 80,000 fish! Let's see, if my math is correct, that's roughly 20,000 fish per mile. That number is staggering. Average size? About 18 inches. How many rivers in the world hold that many fish? And, the best part, the river can be fished 12 months a year. In the past the flows from the dam have been predictable and steady, however the predictability has ended. There is unimaginable controversy among many state and federal agencies, environmentalists, fly-fishing advocates, etc. concerning water flows. It's been going on for a couple of years, with no end in sight.

*This beauty was tested for whirling disease then planted when it was somewhere between five to seven inches.*

*Elk Hair Caddis*

*Goddard Caddis*

# The San Juan Worm

You're not going to win any ribbons at the county fair for tying a San Juan Worm. Nor will you ever see it auctioned at an FFF event or in a shadow box on the wall of someone's den. But if you fish with it, you'll catch a lot of fish. Big fish.

The mere mention of the "worm" can elicit the worst kind of snobbery and disdain. Perhaps if it had a different Latinate name: the San Juan Annelid or, better still, the San Juan Lumbriculidae or Tubificidae, that might help. I suspect that the same people that slam the San Juan Worm will tie on a scud or even an egg pattern or perhaps, an Egg Sucking Leech, never mind that a leech is just a flat, segmented aquatic worm. No matter how euphemistically disguised, a worm by any other name is still a worm. Let's take a brief look at this reviled, fly scientifically and historically.

First, scientifically: According to Bob DuBey, Fisheries Specialist at the New Mexico State University, the San Juan worm belongs to a general class of worms, called Annelids. They include the families Lumbriculidae, Naididae and Tubificidae. There are two worm families we, as fly-fishers, are concerned with in the San Juan River and other western streams and tailwaters.

The Naididae is so small (3/8 inch long) that we aren't too interested in tying a fly to replicate it. The Lumbriculidae and the Tubificidae, however, warrant our attention. The aquatic *Lumbriculus variegates* is closely related to the *Lubricus terrestris* which is an earthworm. Personally, I can't tell the difference. Indeed, earthworms are washed into rivers from their banks during spring run-off. (Which, by the way, is replicated by increasing the flows out of Navajo Dam each spring on the San Juan.) The *Lumbriculus variegates* have a pink skin and are about 3/4 to 2 inches maximum in length. Not 5 inches, these are not the so called nightcrawlers. Now, the other little devil is the *Tubifex tubifex* (Tubificidae). It is actually translucent; it looks red because we see the hemoglobin in its body through its skin. This

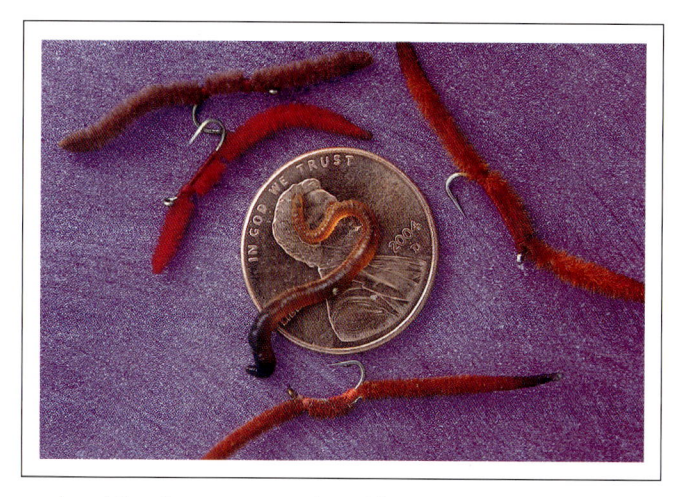

*A real San Juan worm together with some common imitations.*

is one of the hosts for whirling disease, trout are the other hosts. Trout ingest the spores when they eat the worms. These worms are about 1 inch long and very skinny.

The San Juan worms live in the aggregate of moss and algae on top of and under rocks, and in the silty substrate and debris of lakes, ponds, pools and most of the western tailwaters like the San Juan, Bighorn and Green rivers. Typically, the worms feed with their heads in the sediment and their tails pointing upward to the more oxygen-rich water. Because they are not very well anchored, aquatic worms are dislodged and washed into the river's main current on a regular basis. Since they cannot swim, they are reluctant passengers in a catastrophic drift ready to be pounced on by industriously hungry trout. This is true during high spring releases on any western tailwater.

A little history: While having dinner at the Soaring Eagle Lodge, Bob Pelzl, of Albuquerque, NM, told Larry Johnson and me about fishing with his buddy Jim Aubrey in mid-1960. The story goes—even though they threw everything they had, it was a really nonproductive day. In desperation they started to fish a pattern that Jim designed to imitate shrimp in Colorado. It was a rather gaudy-looking thing of umber sparkle chenille tied on a size 10, 4X hook with an over-wrap of red floss at the center. Actually the red floss looks a little like a clitellum of a worm. Without delving into the sex life of a worm: the clitellum

*Bob Pelzl, San Juan Worm originator tying on one of his creations.*

is the slightly thick band around the front half of worms. It's a special organ that helps them carry on reproduction. That's all we need to know.

Bob knew that there were no scuds or shrimp in the section of the river they were fishing. And certainly nothing of an orange color. After examining the contents of a very careful seining, he realized that the "shrimp" pattern was really imitating an aquatic worm. So, the next fly Bob tied on to a number 10, 4X hook looked like a worm. He wrapped a tan-colored yarn body from the bend of the hook to the eye. Then he over-wrapped salmon yarn to suggest a clitellum. The body is tapered at both ends. And voila! A fly is born. Word got out about the success of Bob's "San Juan Worm" and it motivated a multitude of tiers to tie their own versions including variations of the current San Juan Worm—ultra chenille tied on a scud hook.

Fish the San Juan Worm dead-drift close to the bottom being careful that your worm/fly moves at the same speed as the river. Don't allow any drag. You can fish them anywhere and everywhere in the river either with or

*The original San Juan Worm.*

*Richard's Aquatic Worm*

*One of over twenty browns caught by the author on a beautiful Thanksgiving Day with his Richard's Aquatic Worm.*

without an indicator—the strikes are not as subtle as with a nymph, you'll feel most of them. Personally, when I fish a river, I like to high-stick the tailout of a riffle with about a 6 1/2-foot straight-line 4X tippet with one lightly weighted fly and no indicator.

The San Juan Worm works as a very effective so-called attractor pattern with a couple of feet of tippet tied into the eye of the San Juan Worm on point and a midge as a dropper tied to the end. Or vice versa.

Tying a San Juan Worm is simplicity itself: tie a piece of ultra chenille, or vernille, onto a hook of your choice. Finished flies are sold in red, tan, burnt orange, pink, brown or black in most fly shops.

The Tubificidae worm is red (from hemoglobin) and about 1 inch long. The Lumbriculidae worm is a little longer, about 1 3/4 inches. The fly I designed to replicate it is a little more sophisticated and a lot more deadly. It's two-toned: maroon and pink, vernille with red wire.

## MIDGES

The two most important year-round foods in the San Juan are the aquatic worm (Order Lumbriculida, family Lumbriculidae), and midges (Order Diptera, family Chironomidae.)

Why, you may ask, does a big (19-inch plus) trout bother to eat such little-bitty bugs? In a word—availability. The San Juan's cold water does not produce really big stonefly, caddis or mayfly hatches but it sure makes thousands and thousands of midges and aquatic worms available. Since midges and aquatic worms are all over the place all year on the San Juan, trout don't use a lot of energy searching for them or eating them. Midges are known as true flies as are their two-winged cousins, houseflies, mosquitoes and crane flies. They come in gray, olive, green, brown, tan, red and black. Their two wings are shorter than their segmented abdomen, and along with six legs, stem from their muscle-bound thorax. Essentially, they look like mosquitoes minus the long proboscis. Diptera go back to the Jurassic period, some 150 million years ago.

The name Diptera breaks down as *di* meaning two, plus *ptera* meaning wing. Thus, two-wing. What I think is really interesting is in all two-winged flies, the second pair (the hind set) of wings has been lost, and replaced by a pair of tiny knobbed organs called halteres or balancers. The halteres are jointed to the thorax just like the wings; during flight they vibrate up and down at the same rate as the wings: up to an amazing 1000 times a second. (Maybe that's why our British counterparts call them "buzzers.") The up-and-down vibration in one plane, synchronized with the wings, behaves just like an alternating gyroscope resisting any attempt to change direction and providing great in-flight stability for our tiny friends. Insects don't flap their wings like birds.

And midges, tiny as they, are our really big friends. In spite of their diminutive size, midges are the most important insects on the San Juan River. (Some estimates are midges provide over 60 percent of the trout's diet.) There are tens of thousands of them available each day of every month all year.

Watch the water's surface in the quiet areas of the river—the eddies, the river's edges and the current seams. This is where the midges will congregate. If you see a kind of sipping, or bulging or just a few rings on the surface or just the nose of the trout, they are more than likely eating midge pupae just beneath the surface film as the midges start to emerge. Now, if the rises are more energetic such as head-and-tail rises, the trout are after the adults as they start to fly away, or their small clusters.

You'll often see bunches of tiny midges swarming over the water's surface. This swarming behavior is part of their mating strategy. Males swarm around in clusters waiting for females to fly into the clusters to find a mate. Once a male is selected, the two midges pair off. Some species carry out an aerial mating while other species mate on the ground, rocks or water. When the eggs are fertilized, the female flies over the water and dips her abdomen into the water and releases her fertilized eggs. The eggs sink to the bottom, and begin to incubate. Then she dies. The male dies shortly after mating. Remember, adult midges do not bite, or eat for that matter. They exist only to reproduce the species.

*Midge (Order Diptera, family Chironomidae.)*

In a few weeks the eggs hatch. Chironomidae have a complete metamorphosis: starting with an egg, larva (4 instars or moltings), pupa, imago and the last stage is the flying adult. Midge larvae look a little like maggots with distinct body segments. The larvae build an uncomplicated cocoon-like dwelling of algae or debris. They spend most of their time in these tubes in the bottom silt of the river where they feed on algae and decaying plant and animal matter.

Do not be confused by the term, "bloodworms." Bloodworms are not the annelids (aquatic worms) known as "San Juan Worms." The term refers to some of the largest Chironomidae larvae in the family, much larger than their San Juan brothers. Some grow to 25 mm! They are usually found deep in water right on the bottom, and in the sediment of lakes and ponds below the reach of sunlight. Runs that are about seven feet deep and shallow riffles get the most sunlight on the bottom—therefore the most vegetation and bugs. These are very important depths, they're where fish spend most of their feeding time. When little or no sunlight for photosynthesis reaches the bottom and where sunken, organic matter accumulates and decays, the concentration of dissolved oxygen is too low to sustain most aquatic life. The Chironomidae's hemoglobin, which has a very high affinity for oxygen, unlike vertebrate hemoglobin, temporarily stockpiles oxygen. This supply of oxygen allows the larvae to survive in some of the most putrid water on earth. The name "bloodworm" comes from its reddish color. Midges are, indeed, the ubiquitous Chironomidae—not aquatic worms. In short: A worm is a worm and a midge is a midge.

When fully grown, the midge larvae withdraw into their shelter, construct pupal cases, and then morph into pupae inside these cases. These cases are not the architectural wonders of caddisflies. The pupa is a transitional stage between the radically different larva and flying adult. Once this stage is complete, the pupae wiggle out of their cocoon-like dwellings, and rise, head first, resplendent in their pupal shucks, aided by gasses in their abdomens and thoraxes that provide buoyancy, they float to the surface. This trapped gas, of course, makes their bulging cases shiny, almost like a chrome finish; fish key in on these gleaming specks of food. As the pupae rise to the surface the water pressure decreases and the gas expands and helps split open the shucks at the back of their thorax and head. What fly-fishers call a "shuck" is actually a shed exoskeleton that entomologists call an *exuvium*. Now, that little bit of info may or may not help you catch fish, but I know some of you will find it interesting.

The midge pupae rise towards the surface, and when they are emerging from their shucks is when they are the most vulnerable to predation. When starting their emergence to an adult, they hang heads-up in the surface film. They look like a "C" or an "?" as they hang.

Because of the considerable time the emergers are suspended under the surface film, trout can take their time and be selective. Perhaps this is the reason the rises are rather calm. Trout, especially large trout, use as little energy as possible to catch each meal. They actually seem serene feeding on midges. By the way, there are no wings or other appendages protruding from a pupa. Wings and true legs cannot be molted. Only the flying adult has them.

If the pupae are not eaten during their upward migration and subsequent downstream "emergence drift" and succeed in reaching the water's surface film, they don't pop out of their shuck like popcorn. Even though the trapped gas assists in cracking the pupal shucks, the pupal midges still have to struggle and squirm to escape not only their shucks, but also break through the surface film of the water.

When the insects finally break through, they must wait on the water's surface before flying away: their blood is pumped throughout the body and it expands the body and inflates their wings. As soon as the wings are dry they fly off in search of a mate. On the San Juan, hatches will usually be triggered by favorable water temperatures around 10:00 a.m. and about 3:00 p.m.

Here's a bit of information that I found interesting. Most aquatic insects fly upstream when they emerge as adults. They fly upstream, they lay their eggs; the nymphs get caught in a drift and float downstream. It's a dispersal mechanism.

So, let's try and take a fish's perspective. What do they see from beneath the surface? Well, they see shiny bugs floating heads-up, stopping underneath the surface film while beginning their transformation into adults, all the while wiggling around with their various appendages flailing in every direction. There's a clue here. What should your fly look like?

*Richard's Midge Emerger*

## THE PIKE OF NAVAJO LAKE

By all accounts northern pike should not be in the Rio Grande River or Navajo Lake. But they are, probably planted by misguided souls in Colorado's rivers and tributaries, eventually showing up in New Mexico.

Northern pike spawn in early spring. The exact date varies year to year depending on water temperature. Females begin spawning when they're two years old but they do not build nests like salmonoids do. They just scatter their sticky eggs (on average 63,000, but up to 500,000 for a female weighing 25 to 30 pounds) at random, in shallow water where the eggs stick to the rocks, the bottom, or to vegetation. The males then fertilize the eggs. Afterwards, both male and female move on.

Highly territorial, solitary hunters, these animals evolved fit for their work. Northern pike are at the top of the freshwater food chain along with their cousins the muskie. Pike use their very large mouths to swallow their prey whole. Their mouths are lined with backward slanting canine teeth. Their large teeth on the lower jaw are used to spear and pierce the prey. The smaller teeth on their upper jaws are designed to grasp and hold onto their prey. Boys and girls, you don't want to put your hand, wrist, leg or other appendages in there. Pike (like barracuda) often attack a fish from the side. (Tandem hooks work fine.) Once the pike have the quarry in their mouths, they turn the victim headfirst and swallow. For this reason pike prefer cylindrical fish.

Like bass, the pike's most important sense is sight. They have large eyes positioned foreward and upward, perfect for a daylight hunter. They kill most of their prey in daylight. Important to know.

Pike like to hide, unmoving, in weeds or behind rocks and along the sides of points; set eyes on their victim, then, sprint to kill it. The position of their dorsal fin enables a sudden burst of speed. It's way back near the broad, paddle-shaped caudal fin and above the anal fin. This specialized arrangement of these three fins plus their torpedo-like shape enables the pike to curl their body into an S-shape. By quickly straightening out, these fish can move at incredible bursts of speed of over 20 mph from a standing start. I love these fish on a fly rod.

Adult northern pike are largely piscivorous except for the occasional rodent or small duck snack. (I've never seen a duck-fly, but I'm sure there's one out there.) Important for us fly-fishers to know, they will eat perch and bass; but, as previously mentioned, they prefer a more cylindrical fish—like suckers, minnows, and, of course, trout. Think streamers: think BIG streamers.

Pike will occasionally attack and swallow alarmingly large fish. Their jaws are very flexible enabling them to swallow half of their weight whole. There are stories of pike actually choking to death while attempting to eat another pike the same size!

Northern pike are rapacious predators: they are very, very willing to attack and kill just about anything that moves into their territory—including an artificial scam made of feathers and fur. Actually, I think any fly at least six inches long that replicates a cylindrical fish will work. One of the guides on the Lake likes a green and yellow Double Bunny. He fishes it a lot and catches a bunch of pike. His biggest was 20-plus pounds. Not too shabby. It's probably one of the most productive streamers ever invented. However, after the first cast, it is, of course, waterlogged and very heavy, difficult to cast.

I really enjoy tying with natural materials like bucktail, but synthetic materials have two big advantages: they will not absorb water, and they're durable enough to survive at least three takes. Having said that, esthetically, I prefer nice, long bucktail for my Clousers. My favorite color combinations, because they are very productive for bass as well as pike, are chartreuse and white and red and white. Other successful combinations are green and yellow, and any color and black. Always with the darker color on top.

Devise your own fly—make it long and durable with BIG eyes and some movement; remember, you have to be able to take it off the water and cast it. Or, try some larger tarpon flies, they work just fine. For example, Blanton's Fishtail Whistler or a Black Death.

As for fly rods, I use a combination of the same equipment I use for steelhead and salmon or barracuda. That is a 9-foot 8-weight saltwater rod (nice big eyes, easy to cast) with a disk-drag reel. A reel that has a smooth and reliable drag that's easy to adjust is a must. I spool on 150 feet of 20-pound backing for a 7- or 8-weight forward line designed to throw a big fly.

The top manufacturers make special pike/muskie lines, or you can use your bass fly line. Either one will turn your fly over rather easily. There are several leaders that are perfect for "toothy critters" like pike/musky, barracuda and bluefish. All of these leaders have wire tips to prevent pike from biting off your leader. Pike are very slimy; a glove will help you hold the fish while you quickly remove the hook. Remember that the slime helps the fish swim and protects the fish from fungus and bacteria. Please be careful while handling the fish. They may be aggressive animals, but they too can become sick. Finally, you must take a pair of long-nose pliers to remove the

# San Juan River

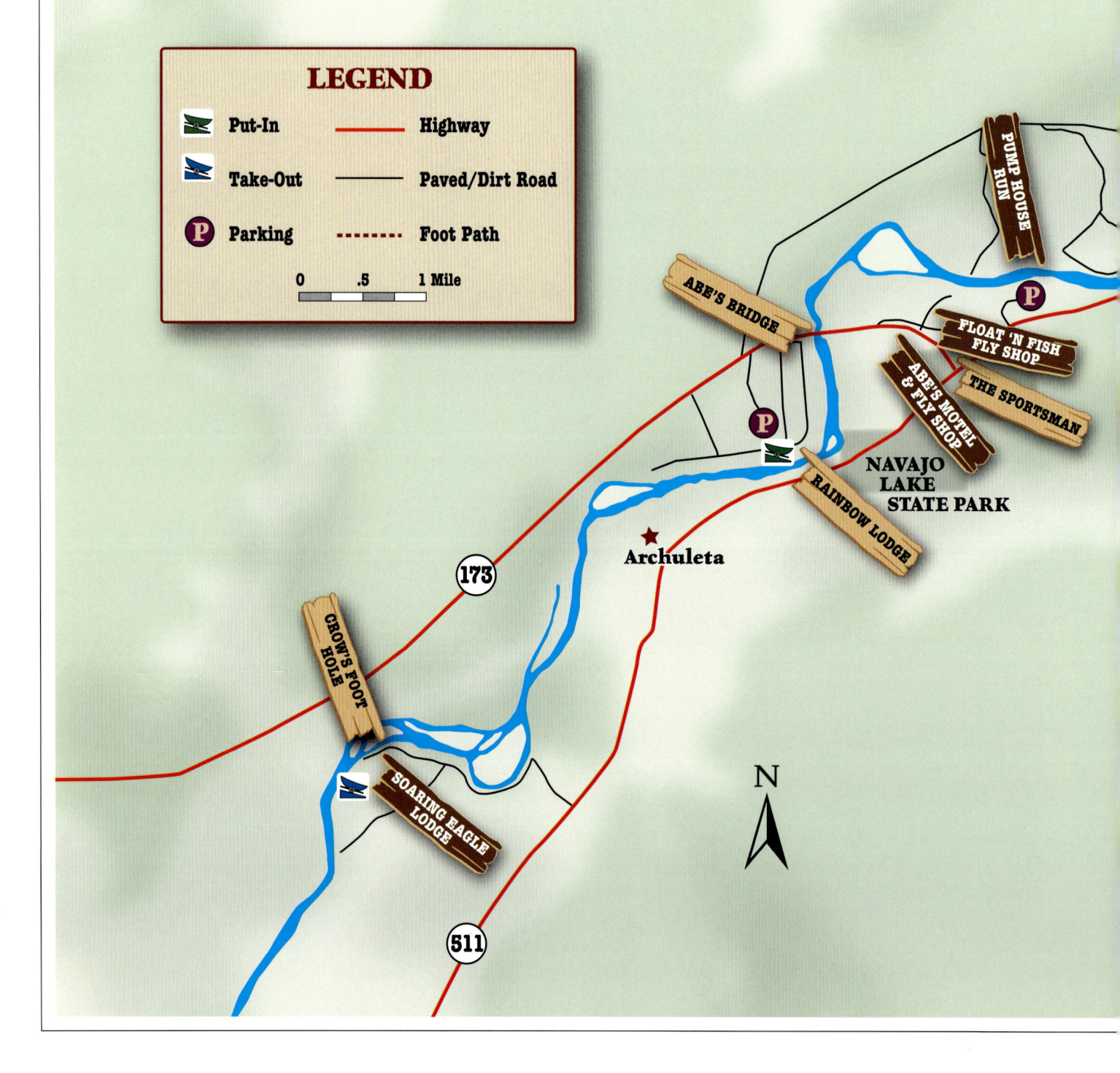

**LEGEND**

- Put-In
- Take-Out
- Parking
- Highway
- Paved/Dirt Road
- Foot Path

0 — .5 — 1 Mile

PUMP HOUSE RUN

ABE'S BRIDGE

FLOAT 'N FISH FLY SHOP

ABE'S MOTEL & FLY SHOP

THE SPORTSMAN

RAINBOW LODGE

NAVAJO LAKE STATE PARK

★ Archuleta

173

CROW'S FOOT HOLE

SOARING EAGLE LODGE

N

511

## Hatch Chart (Flow Dependant)

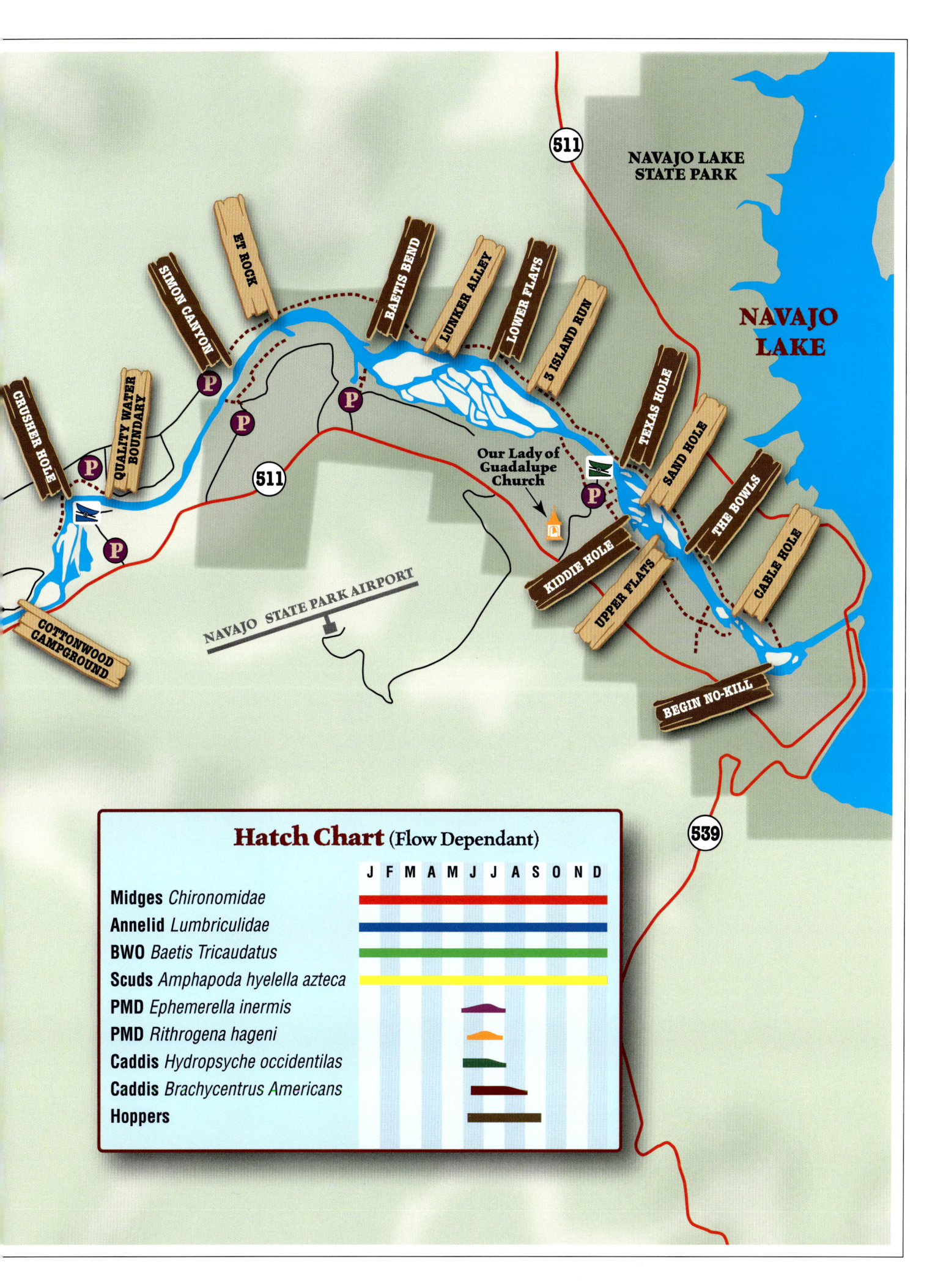

| | J | F | M | A | M | J | J | A | S | O | N | D |
|---|---|---|---|---|---|---|---|---|---|---|---|---|
| **Midges** *Chironomidae* | | | | | | | | | | | | |
| **Annelid** *Lumbriculidae* | | | | | | | | | | | | |
| **BWO** *Baetis Tricaudatus* | | | | | | | | | | | | |
| **Scuds** *Amphapoda hyelella azteca* | | | | | | | | | | | | |
| **PMD** *Ephemerella inermis* | | | | | | | | | | | | |
| **PMD** *Rithrogena hageni* | | | | | | | | | | | | |
| **Caddis** *Hydropsyche occidentilas* | | | | | | | | | | | | |
| **Caddis** *Brachycentrus Americans* | | | | | | | | | | | | |
| **Hoppers** | | | | | | | | | | | | |

hook. I've seen people use jaw-spreaders to hold a pike's mouth open while removing the hook. My personal belief is that the use of a spreader can ultimately be fatal to the fish.

If you cannot see a pike, try casting near weedy areas or alongside or behind the enormous rocks in the lake or the points jutting out from the bank. Pike love to hide there. My goal is to send the fly about a dozen feet past where I think a pike will be lurking. When I retrieve, I want the fly to pass close to these rocks; then I strip at a steady pace. Sometimes fast, sometimes slowly, sometimes I alternate speeds.

In any underwater world, a prey-fish trying to escape a predator in hot pursuit will swim as fast as it can to escape. I don't believe it would stop or slow down, so when you see the pike following your fly, don't stop! Strip faster! The attack on your fly will be ferocious.

It's difficult not to react when your heart is in your throat, but wait two beats before setting the hook—then hold on. The northern pike will run, they will jump, they will try to cut your line by rubbing it against the rocks. They may even charge you. When you finally land these guys, be careful! They haven't stopped fighting. They will still try to bite you. Remember, those teeth can do major damage. If the hook is too difficult to pull out without hurting the fish, cut off the fly and release the fish. They will have a better chance of survival. You can catch them again next year when they're even bigger.

Because they depend on their sharp eyesight to find their prey, pike feed mainly in daylight. Their most active feeding times are: 8:00 a.m. to 11:00 a.m. and 2:00 p.m. to 4:00 p.m., with time out for a nap (theirs) from about 11:30 a.m. to 1:00 p.m. Very convenient.

*Clouser Fly*

*Fooled by a green-and-white Clouser Minnow.*

## Bass of Navajo Lake

Navajo Lake is a lake of canyons, coves and steep-sided points. The mouths of coves and canyons on Navajo Lake are typically wider than their back ends. Depending on the lake's water level, the walls can be massive, sheer vertical cliffs plunging deep below the water's surface. Each cove and canyon has different water temperatures depending on water depth and how much sun the stone walls get to transfer into the water. As a consequence, the lake's fish population is not homogeneous; each cove has its own residents with slightly different spawning dates and feeding times. Search and ye shall find.

The points are like appendages protruding from land and penetrating deep into the water. On each side the water drops precipitously especially close to the tip. Big bass and pike like to hide in the water along the tip and sides of the points because they have some protection when they move: vertically to flee, or to move quickly from the depths into the shallows to feed.

I like to work the shallow water first with a Clouser Minnow whose eyes are only lightly weighted. If I don't get results, I then make a quick change to a deep-diving, larger Clouser for the deeper water of the sides and the point. I guess my "rule of thumb" is if I'm fishing in shallow water and only catching undersized smallmouth, I fish a few feet deeper—more than likely I'll get into some bigger fish. Really big bass live in deep water. They eat and spawn in fairly shallow water, but the time they spend there is minimal and typically during the safety of darkness. So, of course, a great time to fish the shallows for large bass is during the low light of early morning when the majority

*Navajo Lake.*

*Captains Chris Guikama and Rob Degner fishing for, and catching, bass in one of the many unnamed coves on Navajo Lake.*

of smallies will be aggressively feeding. If you like to toss a spun-deer-hair bass bug for top-water action, try dusk. When the sun starts to set, smallmouth will, again, search for food in the shallow water.

Smallmouths seldom go deeper than 30 feet in spring, summer and early fall. However, in late fall and winter, when the water temperature drops below 40° F, activity drops off and they often collect in tight groups down to 60 feet. In late fall and winter, during coldwater periods, they eat very little. They start eating in spring when the water temperature is around 47° F. Depending on the availability of food, the smallmouths' diet will differ from season to season. Even though you caught some smallmouths in September on crayfish, they may be eating insects in May. Smallmouths really depend on their sense of vision more than any other sense for food and survival. Knowing this, I use lures with a natural look. A fishy-looking streamer or a realistic crayfish imitation with a little movement built into the fly.

*The author with another beauty caught on a green-and-white Clouser.*

*Another Clouser-fooled bass, this time it was a red and white.*

Nests built in silty bottoms rarely succeed. Smallmouths need rocks or gravel or hard sand bottoms to spawn fruitfully. When the water temperature hits 60° to 65° F, smallmouths of all sizes usually move into the shallows and start to spawn.

After spawning, her job done, the female bass leaves. The male remains and vehemently protects the nest against any intruders. He will attack anything that gets too close, including much larger fish. Please remember that even though you will definitely catch more bass while the males are aggressively guarding their spawning nests, and even though you practice catch-and-release, be aware that while you're playing a hooked male, a bluegill or crappie will devour the eggs in that male's nest. So, during spawning season consider northern pike, bluegill or crappie.

## CARP OF NAVAJO LAKE

Here, in Navajo Dam, New Mexico, we don't exactly think of carp as royalty, i.e., "the queen of the river," as Isaac Walton put it. Rather, most fishers here call them "Rocky Mountain bonefish." Indeed, there are a few similarities. Carp and bonefish roil about in shallow water searching for food, churning clouds of silt in their wake. The water is often so shallow that their caudal and dorsal fins stick out of the water as they move about, thus the terms "mudding," "tail-

*First light in Spruce Canyon.*

*An average "Rocky Mountain bone fish."*

ing" and "nervous water." Also, both are very, very spooky, darting away at the slightest sound or sight of danger. They both travel in groups or shoals. And they are both known as fighters, bonefish, of course, being the much faster swimmers.

Carp are not easy fish to sneak up on, they can hear better than most fish: they have a lateral line, and they have four or five adapted vertebrae called Weberian ossicles (Weber's Bones) that connect the swim bladder to the inner ear. The swim bladder senses pressure waves (sounds) and transmits them through these small bones to the carp's inner ear. So, the swim bladder acts as a resonator similar to a hearing aid. It's a great system that allows carp to receive a surprisingly wide range of frequencies and they seem capable of determining where sound came from.

Besides having super hearing, carp have a unique warning system. Kind of an alarm. When carp are injured they release a chemical that signals to other carp in the area to swim off and hide. So, if you do manage to hook a carp, the entire area you were fishing no longer has any carp.

One of the days we fished the lake I was mesmerized as we watched carp causing a ruckus splashing and thrashing about in the shallows ahead of us. They weren't feeding they were spawning. I saw them jumping straight up out of the deeper water during spawning for no apparent reason. They looked like tiny, colored whales breaching.

When the water reaches the low 60°s F at the end of May and the beginning of June, groups of carp move into shallow, warm, vegetated waters where they lay and fertilize tiny eggs that adhere to the roots of submerged vegetation.

53

When the water reaches 80 degrees Fahrenheit in the edges of the lake, spawning ends.

Carp feed by wallowing in the mud of shallow water and uprooting plants. Then, using their sucker-like mouths, they gulp the rich organic sludge that they stir up, then spit it out and eat selected items suspended in the water column. Omnivores that they are, they'll sip in any and all emerging and hatching aquatic insects like chironomidae (midges) and caddisflies, and terrestrials like hoppers and carpenter ants, vegetation, seeds, flowers, annelids, small crustaceans, tiny fish, and unfortunately, they will eat fish eggs. They do not have teeth in their mouth. They have well-developed and specialized pharyngeal (throat) teeth designed to grind as do bonefish.

When fishing subsurface in shallow water, look for carp as they search the shallow, weedy, water for food; cast ahead of the target fish with a Woolly Bugger, or Crayfish pattern being careful not to *line* it, let the fly settle, then scoot it along as the carp gets closer and get ready for a great ride.

*The Turck Tarantula*

# Fishing for Carp
## with Chris

When I was a young man I wanted to go fishing with my buddies. Then for a while I wanted to fish alone. Just wanted to be alone on the water. Now I've come full circle; there's nothing I enjoy more than fishing with a friend. After all a little friendly competition keeps you on your toes. Planning a trip together stretches out the trip. The company while traveling to and from the water gives you a chance to catch up with each other's lives. And, of course, the stories about the ones that got away over a drink in the evening. Nice to fish with a friend.

While fishing with a friend (and guide!) on the San Juan, he asked me why I didn't fish the impoundment of the river—Navajo Lake. I didn't have a good reason. As a matter of fact, I had no reason at all. Never really thought about it. My world was always about trout fishing on the San Juan River. So, in the fall of '03 and the spring of '04 I accepted his invitation and Chris Guikama and I fished Navajo Lake off and on for a few months. What a great time. Best to fish with a friend who's also a guide.

We met at the local landmark, the Sportsman Restaurant, Navajo Dam's primary watering hole, at 4:00 a.m. Now, like most everyone, I like to get on the water early. Maybe I'll get lucky and find one of my favorite spots before some guy splashes through it. But getting up at 3:30 a.m. so I could freeze at 5:00 a.m. hurtling through the dark water at 65 mph in a bass boat was unreal. But, that's exactly where I found myself one cold October morning, in a twenty-one-foot bass boat. I never liked bass boats, never will own one, but I came to learn they have a place in the grander scheme of things.

The author thought, "...getting up at 3:30 a.m. wasn't so bad after all."

There's great food on the San Juan—just ask Chef Brad Neuendorf at Chris Guikama's Rainbow Lodge.

As we neared the Colorado border on the San Juan arm of the lake, the New Mexico sun started to warm the thin air—the Lake is at 6,000 feet. We slowed to a stop then Chris killed the 225 horsepower engine and switched to his electric motor. It was quiet, I was starting to like this.

I just finished rigging my brand-spanking-new Sage 9-foot, 5-weight when Chris bellowed, "There're five of them at 11 o'clock about 80 feet. Get ready!" I looked at what he called 80 feet and gracelessly asked if he could please ease up a little and make it 70. After all, it was a new rod, and even though I had cast it on my lawn, I had serious doubts that I could make 80 feet with a 9-foot 5 X tapered leader and a number 10 Turck Tarantula tied to the tip. He did give me, or should I say, he took away, about 10 feet. Just enough.

I tried to predict their path—not any easy task because they zigzagged just like bonefish. I selected one and cast a little ahead of it. Hoping. I let the fly sit where it landed for what seemed like an hour, and then I twitched it just a little. Made the legs wiggle.

The Turck Tarantula is my favorite surface fly for carp. The Chernobyl Ant, Crickets, Stimulators and Big Hair Wing Caddis also work. For subsurface, the good ole Woolly Bugger is great. Clousers work well also.

57

Slowly, little by little, the carp swam over and inhaled the fly. I waited a few heartbeats and set the hook. All hell broke loose and I was into my first carp on a dry fly.

Once hooked, it ran. (Will the knots hold?) I lowered the rod tip to reduce pressure on the rod and line friction on the guides. I let the drag on my reel do the work. I just held on. As it tired, I was able to pull it closer to the surface; once there, I kept turning the carp's head in the opposite direction from where it wanted to swim to disorient it. My brand-new rod was no longer brand-new. It was parallel to the water as I worked it sideways, not holding the rod high above my head. In other words, I played it like any other large, heavy, strong fish: I kept turning its head until it was ready for the net. Chris said the carp came in at about seven pounds. Getting up at 3:30 a.m. wasn't so bad after all.

These are the flats of Navajo Lake. This carp was fooled by a size-12 brown Woolly Bugger.

# Meeting Larry
## — Again

It was mid-morning; I was having a second coffee, (thinking about a second doughnut too) reading the morning paper, and trying to decide where to go fishing. A phone call out of nowhere asked me to come to visit, and, of course, fish 'til I dropped.

It was an old friend. While I lived in Santa Fe, New Mexico the San Juan was my home water for over a decade. Now I live in Oregon and it's always terrific to go back. It will be great to see old friends: Larry, the San Juan and Sunshine.

The last time I saw Larry Johnson was in Boston, Massachusetts. As I remember, he was in an elegant three-piece suit, white shirt and (probably yellow) tie. I remember thinking it was probably custom tailored at Louie's of Boston. At that time, it was the store for well-heeled executives—I didn't shop there. I shopped in Harvard Square. I was in my emblematic Harris Tweed jacket/turtleneck outfit. I couldn't wear jeans that day because we were meeting at Locke Obers Restaurant, just a couple of streets from my studio on Chauncy Street. "Locke's" was (and still is) like a WASPy private men's club—it's like entering a time machine and traveling to a most wonderful spot. Men (and some women) wore suits. I'm sure we both had Indian pudding topped with vanilla ice cream for dessert.

Larry was a big shot in marketing at Polaroid Corporation. I was a photographer/consultant in matters scientific and artistic to Polaroid and others. We were friends. He was off to Photokina, in Cologne, Germany for Polaroid, where many of my works were on exhibit. Eventually he wound up working in the United Kingdom for Polaroid; I later moved to Hollywood for myself. Now he owns the Soaring Eagle Lodge right on the San Juan—I mean, right on the San Juan. I'm retired. I fly-fish a lot, write about it and still do a little photography.

Larry Johnson on the lower river on a typical fall day.

So, what's a fellow to do? I flew to New Mexico, rented a car and drove to the Four Corners. It was dark when I arrived. (I'd have to wait for sunshine.) Inside it was warm and welcoming. Larry was cooking an elk-chile concoction. This time we both had jeans on. We sat and talked over single-malt Scotch (his) and a wonderful Czech Pils beer (mine) poured to perfection—with a one-inch foam head—into a real Pils glass. After we caught up on things personal, we got down to fishing: he told me about his fly-fishing in Iceland, Ireland, Scotland and the trout streams of England; I, in turn, told him about mine in New England, the Pacific Northwest, Belize, the Yucatan, the British Virgin Islands and the U.S. Virgin Islands, etcetera. We were well supplied with Scotch and Pils, the chile smelled great—we were ready for a long night of catching up.

I was intrigued with the method of dry-fly fishing that he picked up on the trout streams of the British Isles. I shouldn't have been surprised, after all, upstream dry-fly fishing was born on the hallowed waters of the Test and the Itchen, two rivers Larry fished.

I asked him how he fishes the San Juan, and what he learned in the UK that can be applied to the San Juan. Larry told me, "The keys to successful dry-fly fishing on

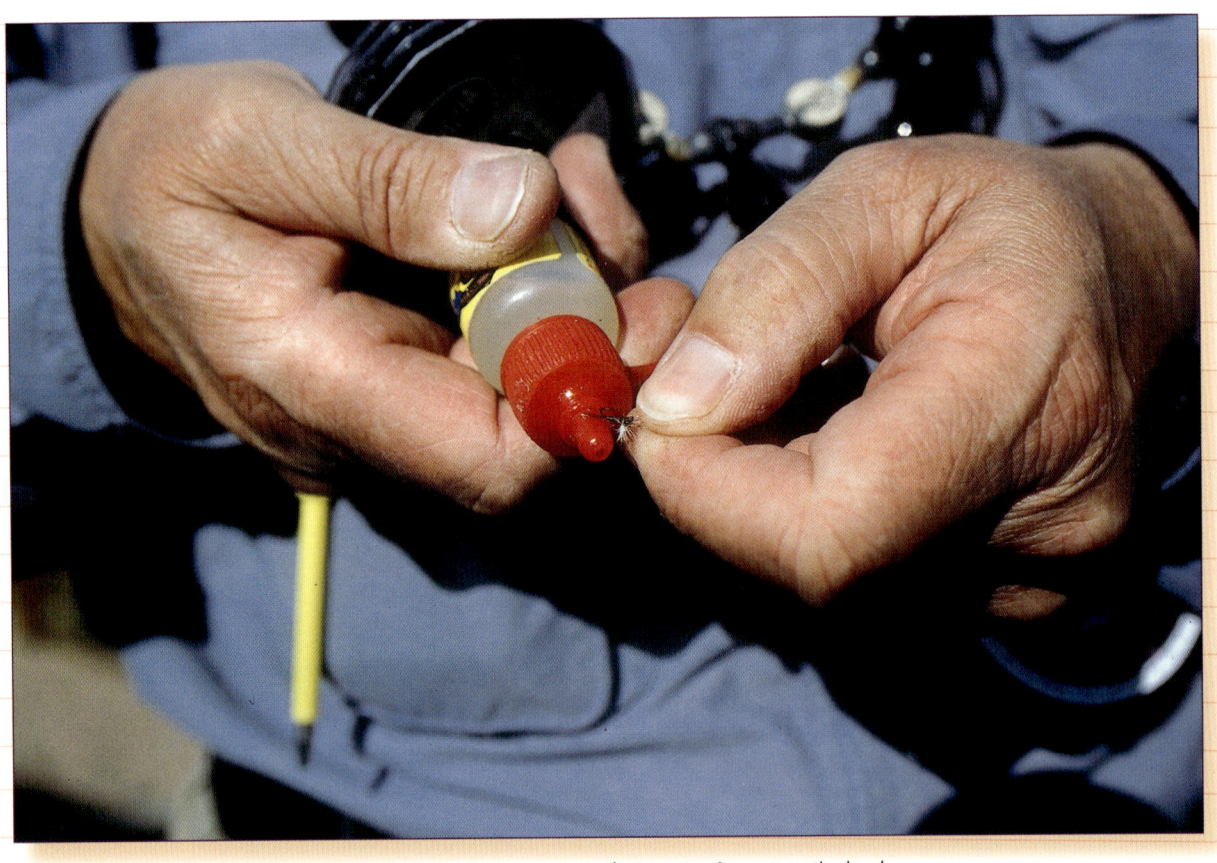

*Larry Johnson skillfully handling a nice brown.*

*Larry Johnson carefully applying Gink to the fly—not to the leader.*

60

Larry Johnson loves casting upstream to a specific trout. The benefit of casting <u>upstream</u> is minimizing drag because the line, leader and fly are all flowing in the same direction in the current. However, he has maximized his chances of "lining" fish.
Larry always presents a very delicate cast and rarely spooks fish. It worked here.

this river—first, you're talking probably a cast of, say, 25 to 30 feet, pretty short; but you've got to put it within an eight-inch zone, completely drag free, right on that fish you're after for him to take it. Second, but just as important, is to mask that tippet. I use a sweet little 8 1/2-foot, 4-weight for most of my dry-fly work."

Larry continued, "When I fish the surface I use a 5X tapered, mono-leader that's about 7 to 8 feet. To that leader I connect approximately 12 to 15 inches of 6X fluorocarbon tippet with a triple surgeon's knot. I use the fluorocarbon tippet because it's a little denser than the mono: I want the tippet to sink. Now, after I've fished for a while, if the tippet becomes buoyant and hinders the presentation—in other words, if the tippet starts to float, I'll treat the tippet with a product called "Mud" sold by Orvis. This stuff comes in a little red plastic flip-top container; I put a little on the tippet right up to the fly—being very careful not to get any on the fly. It sinks the tippet and an added benefit—it reduces leader flash."

I asked why he didn't use an entire fluorocarbon leader to begin with. "Price," was the quick answer. The longer answer was, "For any pro or guide that fishes a couple of hundred days a year, the cost of using an entire fluorocarbon leader is prohibitive, considering he changes tippets after hooking about three fish depending on their size."

Another single-malt and a Pils, and he continued—this time he stood up and demonstrated (sans fly rod),

Larry caught this brown on a size 20 Parachute Adams on his property.

right there in his (rather large) living room. "I cast my fly straight upstream toward a feeding trout. I like casting upstream because there is the least possible drag on the fly. Think about it: the whole rig-line, leader, tippet and fly—is moving with the current at the same speed and in the same direction so there's the least possible drag on my fly.

"The bad thing is I've 'lined' every fish in front of me, it's a problem because the line will drift over their heads. So, I've learned to cast so I have a nice gentle landing. I try to put the fly about five feet upstream from the lie. This way the leader lands on top of the fish and the heavier line is behind it. I rarely spook a fish this way." Chile sure smelled good.

I asked, "Do you guide your clients the same way?"

"For my clients, a lot of times I'll tie a bigger fly—say a size 16, which, by the way, is a big fly for this river—onto the end of the 5X mono-leader; then I'll tie the 18 inches of fluorocarbon tippet to the bend of the size-16 fly. On to the end of the tippet, I'll tie the fly I think will work, say a size 26 Adams. I use two different sizes of the same pattern. Most people can't see the size 26 Adams at 30 feet, but they can see the size 16, and they can follow it. I tell my clients, 'Just think of the larger fly as an indicator,'—they know that the size 26 is about 15 inches away—'if you see that indicator fly move, gently set the hook.'" It must work, his clients return trip after trip year after year.

Fresh, warm corn bread, with creamy Irish butter, and elk chile. My, my. Although I'm sworn to secrecy about the recipe, personally, I think the chiles—both red and green from Hatch, New Mexico—gave his magnum opus sublime qualities. We ran out of Pils and single malt, slept like babies, got up late the next morning, had breakfast; then Larry showed me around the property under a welcoming sun, shining from that beautiful blue New Mexico sky.

Around three o'clock we noticed a Baetis hatch so we geared up and went fishing right in front of the lodge. I tried his tippet method. Simple enough. Caught a few browns and I've been using it for dry flies ever since.

Since that time I've been back at The Soaring Eagle Lodge many, many times. The lodge is about eight river miles downstream from Texas Hole. It has some wonderful water and most important—privacy.

The river pours into a magnificent hole called the Crow's Foot right in front of the lodge. About 1/4 mile downstream there's a small island and the river splits. On the northern bank is the Honey Hole where I've caught some really nice browns. (Are there any other kind?) Downstream another, maybe, one-hundred yards, is Trailer Hole. I've since spent hours at this one hole, using everything from dries to midges and San Juan Worms to Flashback Pheasant Tails and streamers. And landed a bunch of fish. A little further downriver a braid streams in from the northern split. Just let your flies drift from the head of this braid—then, hold on.

The lower river on the Soaring Eagle property.

# A Conversation with Marc Wethington

It was a Friday, somewhere around mid-day, cold, gray, and snowing—too uncomfortable for even the diehard. We had been fishing for a couple of hours. Caught a few fish then decided to get warm and have a sandwich and some hot coffee. We stepped into the Sportsman Restaurant—found a table in the corner—away from the TV sets and juke box, and ordered some burgers—and talked.

Marc Wethington is a biologist with the New Mexico Department of Game and Fish stationed at the San Juan River in the Village of Navajo Dam. He's been fishing the San Juan River since he was six years old. (The man loves the San Juan.) So, my guess is about thirty-years—give or take a few. A tall, unassuming man wearing patches-on-top-of-patches waders. We've fished together many times, and caught a bunch of fish together many times. We each have our own methods—tricks we think are better than the other guy's, but we never really talked a whole lot about them. I'm grateful that Marc took the time to sit with me, over many of cups of coffee (I bought this time), to answer a few questions. Here's part of that little chat.

Q: I know you've been fishing this river for a few decades. Do you guide at all?

A: Yes, I guide part time—have been for 5-6 years.

Q: When you guide, do you prefer to wade or drift?

A: I pretty much wade guide. I haven't really gotten into doing the float trips: I like walking around. I think you learn more about fishing by wading. The floats are good for people who can't walk, don't want to walk. They can catch fish; they don't have to know anything about fishing. If fishing's on, the guide can keep them in the right zone and they can catch fish whether they know anything or not. If I have someone that's new to fly-fishing, I can teach them more during a couple of hours of wading than I can in a couple of days of drifting.

Marc Wethington high-stick nymphing at the Sand Hole. That's the Dam in the background.

Q: What's the most memorable fish you've caught on the San Juan?

A: I've caught a lot of fish that were pretty memorable, but right after I started in this position with Game and Fish, I caught—in one afternoon—and I landed four or five fish that were 20 inches plus. I caught one right at 25 inches that was as nice a looking rainbow trout as you could find. A great big heavy fish.

Q: What did you catch it on?

A: A little black midge emerger, at that time it was about a size 22. I don't remember the name.

Q: When was that, what year?
A: It was as good, and as easy, fishing as you could ask for. I think it was '96; anyway, it was one of the years when we had a high spring runoff, when the water was dropping and the fish were serious about eating. It definitely wasn't tough fishing.

Q: So what's a small fly now?
A: A lot of people fish 26's, 28's, and even 30's, you know. I fish small flies a lot. You're not going to land as many fish on those little flies, but some days you get a lot of hook-ups. To me, the hook-up is the best part; if I land it that's ok, and if I don't, it's ok. I like the strike. A lot of times, fish get off, but that's OK with me—that way I don't have to handle them, I don't have to slow down, I can go right back to fishing, and more hook-ups.

Q: I know you do a lot of nymph fishing. How's the dry-fly-fishing here?
A: Great. I like dry-fly fishing a lot. We have some nice Baetis hatches; you always have midge hatches. Occasionally some caddis depending on the flow, and, of course, midges. Fishing midges as a dry fly is tough; not everybody has the ability to do that very effectively. When we get good Baetis hatches, it's a lot of fun.

Q: What mayflies are on the San Juan?
A: The two primary ones are Baetis tricaudatus, which is your Blue-Winged Olive and the Ephemerella inermis; to a lesser amount there's also Rhithrogena hageni—those last two are your Pale Morning Duns.

Q: When do they hatch?
A: The Blue-Winged Olives, or the Baetis, hatch throughout the year—just about every day, but especially on overcast or gray days. The PMD's are primarily mid to late summer. They vary from year to year: numbers, hatches, etc.

Q: Are the PMD's all over the river?
A: You find them below the Texas Hole. The water is warmer downstream, so the PMD's are more prolific. Water temp has a lot to do with it. The Ephemerella inermis are from Baetis Bend downstream and the Rhithrogena hageni are down from the village of Archuleta.

Making sure the fish is ready to be released.

Marc with an average rainbow. I'm sworn to secrecy about the fly, but I can tell you it was a size-28 Baetis nymph.

**Q:** Talk to me about Baetis.
**A:** Baetis (Blue-Winged Olive). They'll come off periodically throughout the year. We have periods where we get very good hatches. I mean, I've seen super hatches in the winter. I've seen really good ones during snow storms during March.

**Q:** Are the Baetis all over the river?
**A:** Yeah, you'll find them as high up as the Upper Flats but they also increase as you move down. Once you get below the Upper Flats, they start increasing in numbers and size, and that's a temperature-related thing also.

**Q:** Is there a dry fly you use more than any other to imitate the Baetis?
**A:** That Parachute Adams is one that is a pretty good all-around fly for a lot of different things. I like the plain old Comparadun or the Sparkle-Dun, either one of those. I use those a lot, they're pretty easy to tie and they're very effective. You can even see them down to a 20 or 22; you can see them if you really try. Those are probably the three dry flies I use the most.

**Q:** Curtis Bailey likes the Deer's Hair Comparadun, says it's his favorite go-to fly.
**A:** Yeah, I know he likes it. And so do I. I guess he's been guiding here for at least ten years.

**Q:** What about the PMD's?
**A:** Now the PMD's, they're a short window and I'll use different flies for that. A lot of times I'll use a light tan colored X Caddis fly. That's a nice color and they work pretty well so I use that.

PMD Sparkle Dun

**Q:** When is the window for PMD's?
**A:** Probably late June, early July, maybe into early August, somewhere right in there.

**Q:** Do they hatch throughout the river?
**A:** Yeah, as you move downstream, there are bigger hatches also.

**Q:** Let's switch to caddis. I've seen some Little Black Caddis.
**A:** Yeah, Brachycentrus americanus. It builds a pretty small, dark square perfect case. When you pull the bug out, they're pretty light-colored. Kind of a creamy color. When their dark head pulls back into its case, you can't really see it unless you poke around at it. It's a pretty small caddisfly. As an adult it's somewhere in that 18-22 range.

*I found this Brachycentrus americanus (with case) eight miles downstream from Texas Hole.*

**Q:** Are they throughout the river?
**A:** You find a few above the Texas Hole. But, the same phenomenon applies: as the water temperature increases, the size of the bug does also on the San Juan. So, there are more caddis downstream from Archuleta than at Texas Hole, for example.

**Q:** Is there a big caddis hatch?
**A:** There can be mid to late summer. You can have some pretty good caddis hatches. Some years, really good ones and some years, little hatches spread over a long period of time.

There's also another one we have here, it's the Hydropsyche occidentalis—it's medium size—everybody recognizes those. They're the ones that don't build cases; they're everything from olive green to a bright green color.

They don't have a case: they are a free living sort of caddis. You can find the Hydropsyches, from Simon Canyon downstream for the most part. Again that's probably to do with temperature fluctuations. As an adult they're a moderate grayish brown caddisfly. They're very productive—a great food source for fish and they make for good nymph fishing because somewhere there's always some of the immature stage in the water. You can nymph for them any time.

**Q:** What weight and length rod do you use when you fish dry flies?
**A:** I use a 3-wt., 8-ft. 9-inch Sage the light-light series, it's a soft, slow rod. When you're fishing 6X and 7X tippets you need a soft-action rod otherwise you'll break off a lot of fish. I like light rods and soft tips. I usually just get a 7 1/2-ft., 5X or 6X tapered leader. If it's a 5X, I tie about a foot of 6X tippet on. The only time I use a 9-ft. leader is if I'm fishing real deep water and I'm nymph fishing it. I never fish a long leader.

I seldom put any kind of floatant on my tippet. Once you figure out your casting, you should have an idea where your fly is. If you get used to looking at small flies on the water, it gets easier with time. Occasionally I'll fish a big dry and a dropper below it, but if I'm trying to fish just a small dry like a Comparadun, I don't put anything in front of it.

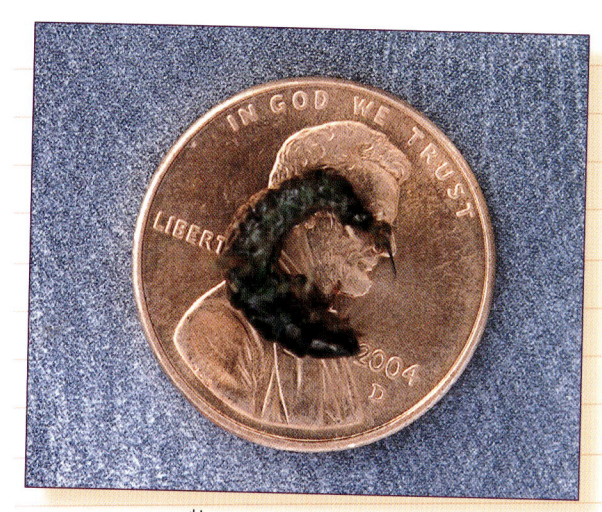

*Hydropsyche occidentalis*

**Q:** What are you calling small?
**A:** Size 20, 22, 24—dry fly.

**Q:** Do you use the same rod for nymphing?
**A:** Yes. Typically I use the same rod for nymphing. Occasionally I fish a Sage 4-wt. SPL. It's the 8-ft. 9-inch SPL.

**Q:** How do you rig for nymphs?
**A:** Again, I use a 7 1/2-ft. leader; I'll use a 4X or 5X leader. The first thing I'll do is I'll tie on somewhere between 14 and 24 inches of tippet the next size down and that's so I can put my weight above that knot where I tie the tippet on so my split shot doesn't slide up and down. I'll tie on my larger fly, and then I'll tie on a 6X for the dropper fly. I usually go anywhere from 12 to 20 inches tippet for my dropper fly. I go kinda long, that way I can change my dropper two or three times before I have to change my tippet.

**Q:** Do you tie your dropper from the eye or from the bend of the hook on your point fly?
**A:** From the eye, typically. There are a few types of flies that I'll use that I'll tie from the bend. If I'm fishing something big like a Woolly Bugger, a Bunny Leech, something like that, I'll tie it from the bend, but for everything else, I tie it through the eye.

PMD Parachute

69

**Q:** What's your favorite hole here?

**A:** There are times I like fishing to fish I can see. So there are a couple different places. I like the main channel above the Texas Hole on the north side especially when the water's around 700 to 800 CFS and you can see fish move up on the sandstone.

**Q:** You're fishing dries up there, aren't you?

**A:** I fish dries and I nymph it both. What's nice up there is if you get a Baetis hatch, the water's fast enough the fish don't have time to really examine your fly. It's either, "I'm going to eat it, or I'm not going to eat it, but I don't have time to think about it." It's pretty quick. Now when you get those fish up on the edge, up on the flat, slow water, now they have more time to think about it. You'll see fish come up, take their time, look at your fly, decide they don't want it, and then just drop down.

**Q:** You and I have fished the Sand Hole a couple of times on the south side, above Texas Hole. It must be one of your favorites also?

**A:** Yeah, it's where all that sandstone is, the south side of the main channel. Those fish'll get up on top of that sandstone and they can be pretty picky. It's kind of funny because you'll watch people go by all day long and they'll stop, fish those fish, and fish those fish, and if they really don't have an idea of how to really fly-fish, if they don't know what they're doing, they're not likely to catch any of them. I don't mind fishing for 20 or 30 minutes to a fish if it's a big fish, or if there's something unique about it. A lot of times you'll walk up and you can see fish and you can tell if they're eating right away.

**Q:** How do you tell if they're feeding?

**A:** Their movements, what they're doing in the water.

Twenty Somethings: At 12 o'clock a Copper John with an Angel Hair tail (shuck); 3 o'clock Flashback Pheasant Tail; 6 o'clock Copper John; 9 o'clock Brassie; Center is a Copper John tied with blue wire and an angel hair tail (shuck).

*Loopwing PMD*

**Q:** For example?

**A:** If the fish is just sitting there stationary in the water, little or no movement just kinda sitting, you could run a dozen different flies over him again and again, if he's just not feeding you're wasting your time. When you walk up and you see fish in that faster water or that shallow, quick water and you can see the fish moving back and forth, back and forth, it's pretty obvious that they're feeding. Those are the easy fish to catch. You can walk up a lot of times and say, "I can catch that fish, or maybe I can't catch that one," and you can walk around and find fish that are easier to catch than others.

Now when I find a big fish or something's kind of unique about one fish in particular, then more effort sometimes is required. I don't have a problem fishing for a fish for an extended period of time if it's the fish I want to catch. It's kind of fun to pick out a fish and either he wears you down or you wear him down. Catching a 30-inch rainbow, I don't care where you're at, it's an impressive fish. Occasionally somebody catches one here on the San Juan that's 30 inches, but it's a rare occasion.

**Q:** We were talking about favorite holes...

**A:** Like I said, I like that main channel by the Texas Hole and I like that shallow kind of quick water where you can walk around and pick fish out—you know, fish to them. The Upper Flats, there's lots of areas where you can walk around and find individual fish. Most of my fishing the last few years has been from the Texas Hole up to the dam. In previous years, I fished more below so the fishing has just changed over time. I've had a lot of different favorite places to fish. Sometimes you get stuck in a rut and you go to the same place over and over and over without really thinking about it just because you get out of the car and that's where you walk to. Force of habit, I guess. Sooner or later, you get stuck in another rut and you go somewhere else for the next six months.

**Walter**, my Australian Cattle Dog (also known as a Blue Healer) hated the water. I mean HATED the water. In spite of this, he loved to go fishing with me. There's a really nice pool between a little island and the main channel of the river near the Cottonwood Campgrounds that I hit each time I fish the San Juan River. On my way I must walk across a little channel on the south side of the river, then walk a little way downstream, wade calf-deep to the island, cross it, and fish the pool. Very easy.

However, with Walter here's how it went: I first waded across the little channel, put my rod down, waded back across the channel, picked up Walter and carried him across. Then we walked together along the shore until we were near the island. Of course I had to repeat the process again to get us off the island. But I'll tell you, when I was up to my butt in water fishing, I looked back and saw that little smiling face watching me—the whole exercise was more than worth it. And besides, he never, ever, commented on my casting. He lived fifteen years with Molly and me—what a blessing.

Cottonwood Campground is on the left bank. In the middle, just above the rapids, is the island that I loved to fish with my dog Walter.

# An Interview with
## (my friend) Bear Goode

Bear Goode is one of the most recognized guides on the San Juan. Not because of his size, which is noticeable, but as one of the most expert guides on the river. Everyone knows this modest fellow of very few words.(Until you get to know him.) By the way, Bear has no fewer than four undergraduate degrees.

Doesn't seem fair, really: A trout has a brain about the size of a pea. (What does that say about the rest of us?) Bear's been guiding for 20 years, give or take. I've been fortunate in having him as a friend and fishing partner. Each time we have gone out we've caught a bunch of fish and had great banter with a lot of laughs—sometimes at ourselves, usually for doing things that we should know not to do. One day I sat down with him at Ray Johnston's Float 'N Fish Fly Shop and asked a few questions. Here is some of that conversation in our own words.

*Bear's tying bench at the Fish 'N' Float Fly Shop.*

**Q:** Why do you like fly-fishing?

**A:** I grew up hunting and fishing. When I was a kid I was always outdoors. Most of the places we fished were for catfish. I didn't even know what a bluegill was until I was 20 years old. Back then it seemed to be the only way my dad knew how to fish was to put something stinky on a hook, throw it out in a lake or a river and just sit there on the side. It was boring. It's not my idea of a fun summer day standing in the hot sun chucking some line out and sitting and waiting for your rod to bend over.

In fly-fishing you can get in the water. You get to see so many more things around you. You are constantly mending your line, my left hand is usually stripping line or trying to give out slack and my right hand is operating the rod. Once you catch fish on a fly that you've tied and give some flies to some buddies who then come back with glowing reports and when fly shops sell your flies and people from all over buy the flies and come in with reports on how well the flies worked, it's an almost overwhelming feeling.

**Q:** Can you give the readers some general principles for fishing the San Juan?

**A:** Here the water's a constant 42-44 degrees year around, actually a couple of degrees warmer in the winter and a couple of degrees colder in the summer. A lot of people are used to thinking the early bird gets the worm. They go out early and fish, then take a long lunch break and they come back in the evening to catch the late hatch. Because a tailwater river is reversed from a seasonal type stream, here the best time to fish is 10 in the morning to 2 in the afternoon or 11 to 3—that's the time in the day where everything's warming up, fish are waking up, the bugs are starting to move.

Most of the hatches don't start until around 10 and then once the bugs start their emerging process moving from the bottom to the top they get a little active on the bottom and start coming up just about everywhere. The midges and the Baetis will both move their way to the

Ray Johnston, Molly Twarog and Bear Goode—
three of my favorite people.

surface. As the fish follow the bugs to the surface, they'll also start eating the adults on top which is the dry fly.

The general rule here on the San Juan is to adjust a strike indicator to 1 1/2 to 2 times the depth of water. Early in my career I was following that rule, but what I was finding was the fish would look up and see my indicator and would follow it, sometimes actually biting the indicator because as they look up it looks black like a little cluster of midges. It's kind of comical when they do take your indicator, but even if they don't, they would follow it for two or three feet. By the time they got back to their original feeding lies, your flies have already gone past them. I think it happens a lot and a lot of fishermen are thinking they're doing everything right, but they're not catching fish. The indicator is either scaring the fish because it's going so close to them or they think it's a midge cluster or a large bug and they follow it as food. The guys who do the 1 1/2 times the depth of the water usually don't change their weights very much. As I switch weights, they're moving their indicators up and down. I don't adjust my indicator to accommodate the depth.

Q: What do you mean by switching weights?
A: I usually start with a 9-ft. tapered 4X leader. I will tie on two feet of 4X tippet to the leader. Above that knot

Big Bear Baetis

74

is where I put the weights (split shot). At the end of the tippet I tie on the first fly and then two feet of tippet to the second fly. That's about 13 feet overall length.

When I say heavy weights I mean: I use 2-3 number 4 split shot (a number 4 split shot is 2 grams) through the day. This is when I'm fishing real deep water, say in 15 feet or more. If we get in water that's 3 to 4 feet, I'll just go down to one number 4. If we're in a riffle that's a fairly deep riffle that has a good current going through there, I might drop down to one number 6 or one number 4. In the shallower riffles, I'll use one number 8-wt., just enough to help it break the surface and not enough so that I get hung on the rocks. That way, I keep the line fairly tight from the weight to the indicator and with the flies below the weight it allows the flies to move around more naturally with the current.

Q: Here we are at Texas Hole—how would you fish it?
A: To start with, in the morning I'll fish real deep; have a total leader and fly length of approximately 13 feet with heavy weights. As the day progresses and the bugs start coming around I'd start fishing more mid-range. Because as the day progresses, the fish have a tendency to move closer and closer to the top and later in the afternoon they'll go back down and suspend. What I mean is, they won't get on the bottom and they're not close to the top so you just have to use different weights (split shot) and experiment to see at what level you get hook-ups. I just run a quick series of experiments of lightening up the weight or adding weight and seeing where the fish are. For example, if I start getting hookups at five feet, that's where I would concentrate my drift.

Q: Do you use a two-fly rig?
A: Fishing the San Juan, we've always fished a dropper. Except for the die-hard dry-fly fishermen, you'll find 99.8% of all fishermen using two flies. In New Mexico, it is legal to use up to 25 flies on a single line. If I'm using something big like a San Juan Worm or a Bunny Leech or a Woolly Bugger, I'll tie off the bend. If I'm using two midges, maybe some RS2's, I usually tie into the eye of the hook so the top fly will actually have two knots into the eye of the hook—one coming from the leader side and one going to the tippet side for the second fly.

Q: When you fish a two-fly rig are the flies different?
A: If the water is off-color and the fishing is not what it should be, I'll start playing around with patterns on the dropper. On the top fly I'll try something like a SJ Worm—I'll try different colors of those, or maybe an egg pattern, maybe a larger leech pattern.

I'll follow that with something small and bright

*Getting ready for a great day at the put-in at Texas Hole.*

like a red larva or an emerger as a dropper behind it because even if the fish don't hit the top fly because it's bigger and/or bright, it's always working as an attractor to advertise for the smaller fly. The fish may see an orange worm on top, swim up to the orange worm, doesn't want that and sees the small midge behind it and goes ahead and eats that.

Q: What's the most memorable fish you've caught?
A: I've been lucky to have guided a few clients to fish that broke the magical 30-inch mark. In March of 2003 I landed the largest trout I know of being caught in the San Juan. It was 31 1/2 inches long, and had a 22 1/2 inch girth, it weighed about 18.5 pounds! This one sticks out because it was a brown, it wasn't a cuttbow or rainbow like the other two. Personally, I've caught fish that have been an inch longer but this one had a tremendous girth, a nice small head and a really big robust body. There were no hook marks, no spawning marks, and no fungus of any kind. It was just a beautiful pristine fish."

Q: Do you use different rods to nymph and dry-fly fish?
A: If I am going dry-fly fishing on my own, I am partial to a 7 1/2 foot, 4-weight bamboo rod that was made by John Channer of Rainbow, Colorado. I don't put anything heavier than a 6X tippet on it. That's my rod. I'll just take it and put some dry flies in my pocket and enjoy the day. When I don't know whether I'm dry-flying or nymphing, I'll stick with the 10-foot, 5-weight rod. There is no way to say this is the perfect rod. All of the higher quality rods are so nice. Probably a 5X rod is the best weight for all-around. It'll throw streamers and it's also delicate enough for the dry flies and anything in between.

When I'm on my own, I like to sight-nymph a lot. That's where you're walking in semi-shallow or clear water and you see the fish on the bottom. You are casting 3-5 feet above the fish and you're actually watching the flies drift over the fish. You can watch the fish take the fly instead of watching an indicator hoping a fish will take the nymph. That's when I do better with a faster-action, long rod. It makes it a little easier for me to mend at long distances.

Q: Talk to me about the "ant fall."
A: I've been told it's a migration. It's a flying ant about a size 14 regular hook shank. It's a pretty robust ant. Usually around the end of June through July — it doesn't last very long. When the ants are flying around and we get a mist or a light rain or, hopefully, a heavy rain, the ants fall in the water and the trout start pigging out on them. It's a beautiful thing. It's just one day in the summer. If we're lucky, we'll get it twice in one week. Just from that one day, we'll be able to fish ants three to four weeks afterwards.

Scanning the surface before we rig up.

# A Day with
## Tom Knopick

When I stepped out of the Strater Hotel I was slapped hard in the face with a sudden ice-cold wind. Like a blind-sided left hook. It hurt. The October sun was just climbing over the mountains, not doing its job yet—it was early and it was freezing. It was a good time of day to be in Durango, Colorado.

I love this hotel; built in 1887 with red, native brick on the outside, only four stories tall. You can climb the stairs to your room and not even be out of breath. I feel like I'm in a living Victorian museum with a good bar.

I turned left on Main Avenue and walked the two and a half blocks to Duranglers Fly Shop. I was going to meet with Tom Knopick and Barley. (Tom is co-owner, with his partner John Flick, in the shop.) We had planned this trip for few months: a day's fishing on the San Juan—drift a little and wade a lot. Catch a few fish. We talked for a few minutes. Set some goals. I smelled coffee brewing in the back of the shop. On our way out, I grabbed a cup (black with a little sugar), to ward off the evil winter spirits.

The 50-plus miles sped by, moving south from Colorado's irrigated farmlands to New Mexico's high desert where oil and natural gas are the preferred crops. It was a great time for Tom, Barley and me to get to know each other a little better. I finished my coffee. Barley rode in the back seat of Tom's truck just as he's done countless times as Tom's fishing

The Strater Hotel, Durango, Colorado. It's like stepping into the past.

partner. Some of the San Juan guides call him "ole white face" because he has a very, very, light coat for a yellow lab.

We put in at Texas Hole, Tom rowed across the

river then upstream. We beached at a little island formed by a small channel on the north side and the main channel on the other. We three walked up above Texas Hole to an area Tom called the Back Bowls for the many deep bowl-like indentations in the bedrock. This section is in the main channel from the top of Texas Hole upstream to the upper flats. We fished the main channel as it spilled into Texas Hole.

*The Durango & Silverton Narrow Gauge Railroad that operates between Durango and Silverton, Colorado.*

The first fly Tom tied on was a number-12 Royal Wulff. As I watched, a couple of casts and—wham! He hooked up with a nice fish. So much for matching the hatch. Then he tied on a grasshopper. A couple of looks, a few flashes, but no takes. Barley watched.

We could see fish in the thin water, maybe 2 1/2 feet deep; the sun was high and the angle was perfect so when the fish were moving around we could see them clearly eating pupae.

Tom decided to change from a dry fly to a nymphing rig. Habit kicked in and Tom put on a two-fly rig just like most people that fish nymphs on the San Juan regularly. To a 7-1/2' 5X tapered leader he tied on an additional 12" of 5X fluorocarbon tippet, to that he used an improved clinch knot to tie on size-20 red larva pattern; to the eye of the larva hook he tied an additional 12" of 6X tippet, to the end of the 6X he tied on a size-24 midge pupae dropper, again using an improved clinch knot.

Tom told me, "There's a lot of ways to set up a two-fly rig. To a fly that's small, I tie onto the eye of the hook just because I don't feel comfortable having anything around the bend of a small hook. I'm afraid of deflecting a hook-up. If I were fishing a big hopper and, say, a bead-head dropper, I'd probably go off the bend of the hopper's hook because it's a little quicker to tie on and this in-line method has the fewest wrap-around foul-ups. I think for most of us, if we can get the tippet in the eye of the hook, it's easier than tying to the bend of the hook. An 'improved' clinch knot works either way."

We could see a couple of nice fish in a little pocket. Because the fish were visible, Tom decided to fish it without a strike indicator—not because it's the best way to catch the most fish, but just because it's a fun way to nymph. Actually, Tom thinks that for most fishermen a strike indicator is the best way to catch the most fish. Because Tom is such a capable fisherman he has many options in the way he fishes. The choice of using an indicator or not, whether to go subsurface or not, weather to nymph or dry-fly fish, or whether to use a dropper or not, are personal choices.

Tom fishing in the Bowls. (We both like this area.) That's Texas Hole just to the left of the picture.

This is on the north side of Texas Hole. Tom is getting ready for our short walk up to the Bowls.

Look but don't touch. Barley checking yet another beautiful rainbow.

dry—it's just the way I feel. Or, I want to catch as many fish as I can and I'll pick a technique I think is the most appropriate. Once I get a feel of what's happening—it's all choice."

Tom continued, "It's hard to fish these tiny dry flies. Because not all fishermen can see the small flies, they get frustrated. Accuracy of the cast is so important, fish are not going to eat it every time you get close to them so you have to repeatedly put it in their face—it's not easy to do.

Tom again, "There are lots of ways to approach the river. First, before you cast, or even tie-on, look around, find some fish to watch. You'll get a better idea on what to choose. Sometimes all I want to do is catch a fish on a

"On the San Juan, the dry-fly fishing is very technical; the nymphing is in some ways, but the presentation isn't that technical. You get a dead drift and you set the hook a lot. Watch the indicator. When in doubt,

Under Barley's guidance.

set the hook. On the San Juan the fly selection is also pretty technical, novices to experts can be challenged. A guide can put a good angler in a situation that can challenge every skill he's got or you can put someone who's never seen a fly rod in a situation and be very successful."

While on the north side of the back channel, Tom told me to look at some of the other people fishing near us: everyone we saw had his eyes glued to his strike indicator. There's nothing wrong with that.

It was around mid-day when the BWO hatch came off. We had drifted to the south side of the lower end of Texas Hole. We saw a couple of fish about sixty feet away. They were waiting in the quiet water of the seam, then they moved into the faster water now and then to grab an emerger all the while watching for a meal on the surface.

A 7 1/2-foot leader with an 18-inch 6X fluorocarbon tippet and at the business end a size-20 BWO Sparkle Dun.

*One of many.*

But we saw a half-dozen or so different fish rise in just a couple of minutes. Because they were so intent on fishing nymphs (and catching a couple of fish) I guess the other fly-fishers just weren't looking for anything else. There was a BWO hatch going on all around us. Barley looked bored.

Now, I can cast pretty well—seventy feet is not a problem—and I can usually put a fly in at least a three-foot square at that distance. But, I must admit, watching Tom cast made me feel just a tiny bit self-conscious. I knew he had won individual honors in the "One-Fly" contest in Jackson Hole in 1987. His partner,

81

John Flick, won the previous year. But I didn't expect this level.

His casts were perfect. I mean perfect! Forget getting the fly into a three-foot square: he was consistently in a one-foot square, right into the feeding lane. Right on their noses.

Fishing with Tom can be intense, but well worth it—he's definitely one of the great fly-fishers and teachers of our sport.

Tom drove me to my friend Larry's lodge. I had a great day. Molly met me at the lodge. I was going to have a great night—good friends, good food, good stories and great memories. What else is there?

Tom's fly box. I must admit mine is not so orderly.

Tom and Barley, inseparable best friends for years.

# FLY RECIPES

### Richard's Midge Emerger
**Richard R. Twarog**

**Hook:** Dai-Riki #135 Scud size 24 to 20
**Thread:** Black 14/0 Gordon Griffiths
**Tail:** Angel Hair, Pearl blue
**Rib:** Extra small silver holographic tinsel
**Body:** Abdomen black thread
**Thorax:** Peacock herl
**Hackle/legs:** Black saddle hackle
**Post:** Rainy's parachute post equivalent

Note: I designed this fly to be fished in seams and along the edges of rocks in slow moving water. I use a tapered leader of no longer than 7-1/2 feet and I tie the emerger on with a Non-slip Mono Loop knot. Actually I use a short leader each time I fish subsurface. I feel it puts me in close contact with the nymphs and enables me to respond quickly to strikes. In fast water I shorten my leader to about five or six feet.

### BWO Comparadun
**Al Caucci and Bob Nastasi**

**Hook:** Dry fly sizes 22-18
**Thread:** Green 8/0
**Wing:** Mottled brown deer flared upright
**Tail:** Stiff hackle fibers
**Body:** Superfine green

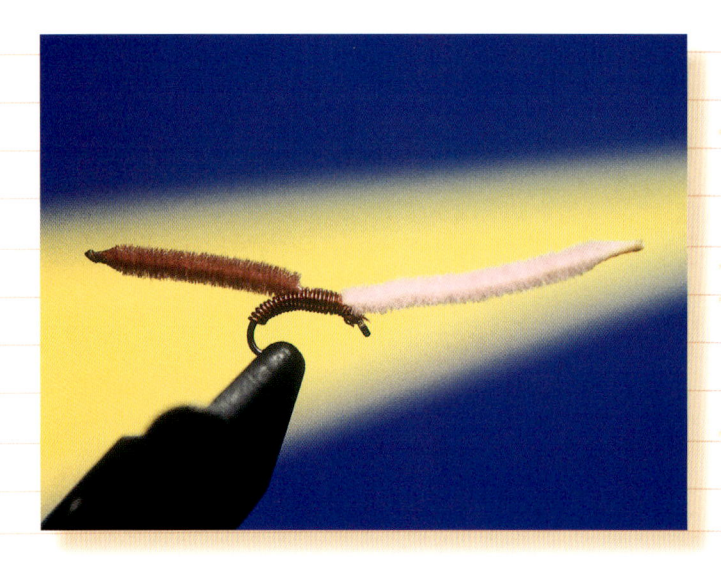

### Richard's Aquatic Worm
**Richard R. Twarog**

**Hook:** Dai-Riki Scud Hook sizes 16-14
**Thread:** Red 6/0
**Body:** Ultra Chenille or Vernille pink and maroon
**Clitellum:** Red, small or medium or large red wire

Note: The size and amount of wire represents the Clitellum and acts as weight. I caught 20 browns on this fly one Thanksgiving Day on the lower river.

### Goddard Caddis
**John Goddard and Cliff Henry**

**Hook:** Standard dry fly size 16
**Thread:** Tan 6/0
**Body:** Caribou or soft deer hair
**Antennae:** Brown or other color stripped hackle stem
**Hackle:** Brown or your choice

### Batwing Emerger – PMD
**Tracy Peterson**

**Hook:** TMC 2487 Sizes 20-16
**Bead:** Gold glass bead
**Thread:** Cahill 6/0 UNI-Thread
**Abdomen:** Turkey biot dyed PMD
**Thorax:** Beaver dubbing PMD
**Wing:** Dyed dark dun hen aftershaft feather

### Clouser Style Fly

- **Hook:** Owner Jig Hook, size 3/0
- **Thread:** I use fine nylon—I like the way the two colors of the head show through.
- **Eyes:** Dumbbell
- **Middlewing:** Silver Angel Hair
- **Underwing:** (belly) White bucktail
- **Wing:** Red bucktail
- **Throat:** Red marabou
- **Head:** Sally Hansen's Hard as Nails

### Big Bear Baetis
#### "Bear" Goode

- **Hook:** Dai-Riki 270 or Tiemco 200R sizes 24 to 16
- **Thread:** Light Cahill UNI-thread 6/0, dark brown for the head 8/0
- **Tail & Abdomen Back:** Natural pheasant tail
- **Rib:** Light cahill thread
- **Body & Thorax:** Thread
- **Wing Case & Legs:** Black Z-Ion or Antron

Note: Bear tells me this fly-fishes best in riffles on overcast days—especially from fall to late spring.

### Loop-Wing PMD

- **Hook:** TMC 100 size18-16
- **Thread:** Tan 6/0 UNI-thread
- **Tail:** Natural dun coq de leon fibers
- **Abdomen:** Turkey biot dyed PMD
- **Wing:** Dyed cream turkey flat (looped)
- **Hackle:** Light ginger

### The Turck Tarantula
#### Guy Turck

| | |
|---|---|
| Hook: | Tiemco 5262 or Dai-Riki 710 size 14-4 |
| Thread: | Tan 3/0 |
| Tail: | Amherst pheasant tippets |
| Body: | Hare's mask fur dubbing |
| Wing: | White calf tail topped with pearlescent Accent or Krystal Flash |
| Legs: | Double strand of brown rubber, medium |
| Collar/head: | Spun deer hair |

### Flashback Pheasant Tail
#### Frank Sawyer

| | |
|---|---|
| Hook: | Standard wet fly |
| Thread: | Olive or brown 6/0 |
| Tail: | Olive or brown pheasant tail |
| Back: | Pearl Flashabou |
| Rib: | Copper wire |
| Abdomen: | Olive or brown pheasant tail |
| Wingcase: | Pearl Flashabou |
| Thorax: | Peacock herl |
| Legs: | Olive or brown pheasant tail |
| Head: | (Optional) copper wire or bead or thread |

In brown sizes 16 or 18, good imitation of PMD. Hatch often begins around 10:00 or 11:00 a.m. In olive sizes 16 or 18, good representation of Baetis.

### PMD Parachute

| | |
|---|---|
| Hook: | Dry fly sizes 18-16 |
| Thread: | Yellow or green 6/0 |
| Wing: | White calf tail parachute style |
| Tail: | Blue dun Micro Fibetts |
| Body: | Chartreuse/green fine dubbing |
| Hackle: | Light ginger or blue dun parachute style |

Note: This fly is very effective from Baetis Bend downstream.

### PMD Sparkle Dun
**Craig Mathews & John Juracek**

- **Hook:** Dry fly sizes 22-18
- **Thread:** Yellow or green 8/0
- **Wing:** Gray deer flared upright
- **Tail:** Olive brown Z-lon
- **Body:** Greenish olive dubbing

### Parachute Adams
**Ed Schroeder**

- **Hook:** TMC 100, sizes 14-22
  Dry fly 22-20
- **Thread:** Black or gray 8/0
- **Post:** White calf tail
- **Tail:** Brown and grizzly hackle fibers (Tracy Peterson used moose mane for this fly.)
- **Body:** Gray muskrat or Superfine
- **Hackle:** Grizzly and brown, (one or two stems of each) wound parachute style

### Elk Hair Caddis
**Al Troth**

- **Hook:** Dry fly sizes 20-16
- **Thread:** Tan 6/0
- **Rib:** Fine gold wire
- **Body:** Hare's ear dubbing
- **Hackle:** Medium brown palmered
- **Wing:** Cream elk hair

### Copper John
**John Barr**

| | |
|---|---|
| Hook: | TMC 5262 or equivalent, size 22-20 |
| Bead: | Brass |
| Weight: | Lead wire |
| Thread: | Black 6/0 |
| Tail: | Brown goose biots |
| Abdomen: | Copper wire |
| Wingcase: | Thin skin, pearl Flashabou and epoxy |
| Thorax: | Peacock herl |
| Legs: | Hungarian partridge or hen back |

### Griffith Gnat
**George Griffith**

| | |
|---|---|
| Hook: | Standard dry fly sizes 16-22 |
| Thread: | Black 8/0 |
| Rib: | Thread or fine gold wire |
| Body: | Peacock herl |
| Hackle: | Grizzly, palmered |
| Post: | Black Antron (optional) |

### A K Callibaetis
**A K Best**

| | |
|---|---|
| Hook: | TMC 100 sizes 18-16 |
| Thread: | Tan 6/0 UNI-thread |
| Tail: | Natural dun coq de leon fibers |
| Abdomen: | Sandy dun quill |
| Wing: | Dun hen hackle tip |
| Hackle: | Light dun |